D1634052

PELICAN BOOKS

A251

ANIMAL PAINTING IN ENGLAND

BASIL TAYLOR

BASIL TAYLOR

ANIMAL PAINTING IN ENGLAND

FROM BARLOW TO LANDSEER

PENGUIN BOOKS

Penguin Books Ltd, Harmondsworth, Middlesex

U.S.A.: Penguin Books Inc., 3300 Clipper Mill Road, Baltimore 11, Md

CANADA: Penguin Books (Canada) Ltd, 47 Green Street,
Saint Lambert, Montreal, P.Q.

AUSTRALIA: Penguin Books Pty Ltd, 762 Whitehorse Road,
Mitcham, Victoria

SOUTH AFRICA: Penguin Books (S.A.) Pty Ltd, Gibraltar House,
Regents Road, Sea Point, Cape Town

—

Published by Penguin Books 1955

FOR

C.H.T.

Made and printed in Great Britain
by Hunt, Barnard & Co, Ltd
Aylesbury

CONTENTS

FOREWORD

THIS essay was originally completed in 1951 and the material has since been slightly extended and revised for present publication. I should like to thank all those who have allowed pictures in their possession to be reproduced and, especially, those who have furnished information about them. It has not been possible to trace the present whereabouts of every work and those owners whose names are not mentioned will, I hope, accept this acknowledgement. I am particularly grateful to Miss E. M. Gilbert and Miss H. Mole of Messrs Arthur Ackermann and Sons for their most generous assistance in finding certain illustrations.

LIST OF PLATES

IN COLOUR

IN BLACK AND WHITE

ANIMAL PAINTING IN ENGLAND

FROM BARLOW TO LANDSEER

ENGLISH has no equivalent of the French *animalier* to characterize the kind of artist considered in this essay. The terms 'sporting art' and 'sporting artist' are too narrow to include all their activities and I have deliberately avoided them, using instead the words 'animal painting' and 'animal painter'. The artists with whom I am concerned have never received their due attention, not even the best of them – Barlow or Wootton, Stubbs or Gilpin, Marshall or Ward. They have had an insignificant place in the canon of English art. When Joseph Mayer, in 1879, sixty-three years after Stubbs's death, wrote the first account of that painter's life and work to be published, he began his essay with these words: 'The name of this eminent artist is familiar to few people at the present day. In some great mansion, the housekeeper will pronounce it, and a visitor who catches that unknown monosyllable in the midst of her drawling roll, may glance with admiration at the big picture overhead, but will probably again forget.' And the same opinion would have been appropriate fifty years before. Stubbs is not mentioned in Allan Cunningham's *Lives of the most Eminent British Painters* published in 1823. Ruskin never referred to him in all the profusion of his writings, and in 1934 Roger Fry, lecturing on British art during the winter exhibition at the Royal Academy, where the painter was not unfairly represented, mentioned Northcote, Opie, Cotes, found a page of approval for Cox, two for Morland, and four for Wilkie, but no word for Stubbs – or Barlow, or Marshall, or Ward.

The rediscovery of the tradition was begun in the eighties by Sir Walter Gilbey in his volumes on animal painters and continued in this century by Walter Shaw Sparrow, but the revival was made in the cause of sport, those pictures which illustrate the history of racing, hunting, or shooting being generally preferred; and this preference still regulates the price of a Stubbs or a Marshall in the sale room or the dealers' galleries. This has recently led Mr Ellis Waterhouse in his *Painting in Britain 1530–1790** to remark, 'To discuss the Sartorius tribe and such painters is no business of the historian of art, no matter how bitter the accusations of neglect are wont to be from those specialist writers who sometimes confuse the history of art with praising famous horses.' This essay attempts to offer an alternative line between the two different streams of neglect.

I would claim, first of all, that this is the only tradition in English art which can claim to be unique, for no other school has produced such an abundance and such a variety of animal painting. These two hundred years saw, besides the continuance of many existing sports, the emergence of fox-hunting and racing and, consequently, the systematic breeding of the thoroughbred, the hunter and the foxhound. They saw the foundation of modern biological and zoological study, the true beginnings of comparative anatomy and the scientific improvement of farm livestock in all its varieties. They saw the growth of a new enthusiasm for country life and an entirely new attitude to the animal creation in general. In no other country were conditions so appropriate for a school of animal painters and nowhere else were the demands met by such a vast and popular output. This tradition is one in which the peculiar situation of the English artist can very clearly be studied. The history of our painting is, when all is said and done, an account of the work which English conditions have required and inspired, which English painters have produced;

**Penguin Books*, 1953.

and that history depends very deeply upon the distinctive and unusual character of our national patronage. English patrons, particularly during the period of this essay, required from native artists a clear, accurate and informed statement of what was to them socially valuable or worthy of commemoration. They wished for a descriptive rather than an idealistic or aesthetic art; they were more likely to be connoisseurs of objects than of *objets d'art*. The physique of most English pictures has been determined by this demand for a descriptive document; the typical English picture is the portrait whether it be of man, animal, or landscape.

The historian of art whose interests and training have been controlled by a study of continental conditions and the sequence of continental styles may well find uninteresting, even unimportant what is, in fact, most characteristic of English art. Stubbs or Marshall have hardly any connexions with Italian, French, or Flemish painting, but they are most typical and important representatives of their own school. A proper history of English animal painting has yet to be written and would require the most laborious and often aesthetically unrewarding research, for, like the explorer among our seventeenth-century portraits, the student would need to have an easy tolerance of inferior pictures. (It is, apparently, more rewarding to deal with bad human than with bad animal portraits.) I have not attempted here to write even the synopsis of that history, but have instead tried to establish the identity of the tradition so that its relationship to English art in general may perhaps be better appreciated. I have not given the essay a chronological form as that has not seemed appropriate to its length, and because I have wanted to distinguish the variety of the animal painter's work. I have not hesitated to surround an account of the pictures with much contributory evidence from outside the history of art. After considering the origins of the school, the career of Francis Barlow, and the most decisive contribution of Stubbs's *Anatomy of the Horse*, the various types of animal picture are then examined separately. Short biographies of the artists represented are given, not in the main body of the text, but in the notes to the plates, and the choice of these has been very much influenced by the problem of reducing a painting to the scale of the book.

As our native school of painting emerged in the seventeenth century several forms of animal painting were accessible and popular in Europe, most of them serving either the traditional interest in the chase and in blood sports or man's constant curiosity about wild animals. There were the hunting scenes of Rubens, Snyders, or Fyt, and, associated with such paintings and with hunting tapestries, the continental ancestors of our sporting prints, published independently or illustrating texts on venery. Among the series which must have been known in England in Francis Barlow's lifetime were the 103 plates by the Flemish-born artist, Giovanni della Strada (Stradanus) entitled *Venationes* (1578), which figured not only forms of hunting common in sixteenth-century Europe, but contests between wild beasts, a favourite subject, and such exotic occasions as *Elephant hunting by Troglodytes in Africa* and *Ostrich hunting in Africa.* Stradanus's Italian pupil, Antonio de Tempesta, also published many prints in the manner of his master, including a series entitled *Ucceliera* (1622) and a *Venationes ferarum, avium, pisium* (1605). Another famous set of hunting prints, in a less courtly style, was Hans Bol's *Venationis, Piscationis et Aucupii Typii* (1582), among whose forty-eight plates are such subjects as *Thus the mighty elephants gather in a herd in hollows with a great noise and are captured at the point of the spear.*

Besides these dramatic and often fanciful subjects representing the chase, there were the modest horse and cattle pictures of Dutch painters like Potter, Cuyp, or Berchem, which were also known through etchings and engravings. And such Flemish artists as Hondecoeter, Boel, and Bernaerts served the fanciers of wildfowl and wild animals by making decorative paintings to set beside the flower and fruit pictures of the time. Among the foreign artists living in England during the seventeenth century were several animal painters, including Abraham Hondius, who worked in the manner of Hondecoeter and died in London in 1695, and Wootton's master, Jan Wyck, whose production included battle scenes similar to those of van der Meulen or Wouvermans. The first native artist to join this tradition was Francis Barlow.

Those who determine not to conjecture and guess, but to find out and know, not to invent fables and romances of worlds, but to look into and dissect the nature of this world must consult only things themselves.

FRANCIS BACON

BARLOW made paintings, drawings or prints of all those sports popular in his time. He published the first pictorial record of a horse race which has survived. He made compositions of wildfowl and other birds in the manner of Hondecoeter and illustrated *Æsop's Fables*, a favourite book of these two centuries. He drew or engraved many varieties of wild and domestic animals and birds, and in a big decoration made for Denzil Onslow he anticipated the farmyard subjects of Morland or Herring. In being the first of his profession in England, he engaged in almost all the activities of his successors.

Barlow was an excellent observer, more faithful indeed than any other native painter of his time to the world of the new science and the Royal Society. From the evidence of his work we may guess that he was at least as interested as Sir Thomas Browne in the structure of a camel's hump or the way in which an elephant bends its knees, but he was not, any more than Browne, entirely released from earlier superstitions, in his case from the animal creation of Gessner's *Historia Animalium* or Topsell's *A Historie of Four-footed Beastes* wherein a horse and a unicorn, an elephant and a gorgon could live together, wherein the traditions and legends of the medieval bestiaries mingled with the evidence of rational observation. If Barlow probably would not have believed in the phoenix, he did confidently reinterpret the ancient story out of Pliny of the battle between the elephant and the rhinoceros (Plate 6); and there is in his work that union of old and modern references which is so typical of a time when the plaintive Mandragora or the virgin-hunting Monosceros could still furnish powerful and suggestive images. He worked most successfully, however, with the common creatures of the English landscape. His native birds and insects, his rabbits, hares, and frogs are his most satisfying creations. A lion, an elephant, a rhinoceros, even an ostrich, all of which he could have seen during his career, in menageries or raree-shows, were still exotic. In his account of them, it seems as though he did not trust the evidence of his senses. In his lifetime the anatomist Tyson felt bound to prove that the specimen of a chimpanzee upon which he based a study was neither a pygmy variety of the human species nor one of the common monkeys. Barlow could not present what was rare and unusual with that confidence which Stubbs brought to reconstructing from skin and skeleton the first kangaroo ever seen in Europe.

Barlow was not like Stubbs an original artist; the methods and mannerisms of the contemporary Flemish animal picture are too obvious in his work, but just as Dobson, by reason of his own observation and sympathies, had given a local character to the continental baroque portrait, so Barlow was not merely a provincial follower of Flemish art. He is the most English of seventeenth-century painters in his understanding of country life. His landscapes belong unmistakably to that succession which was to be crowned by Constable and

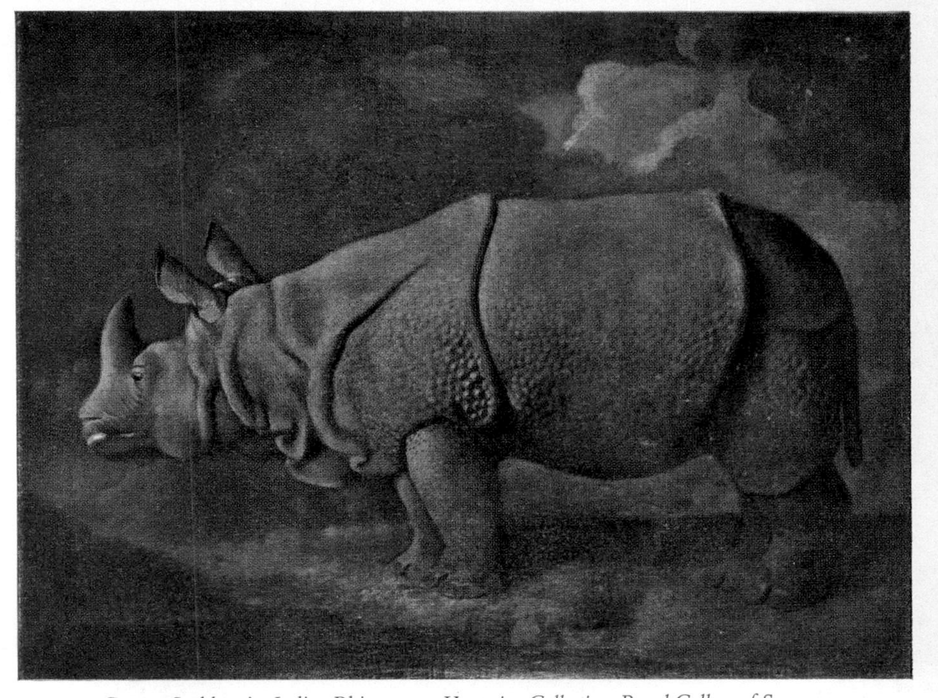

George Stubbs: An Indian Rhinoceros. *Hunterian Collection, Royal College of Surgeons*

Turner; in his sensitive relating of a landscape to its animal inhabitants he is rivalled only by Bewick. Neither he nor Bewick show an excess of sympathy for the animals they record, for both were, in different ways, naturalists and both were born on the right side of that romanticism which will be considered in a later part of this essay. Barlow was remote in time and circumstance from the temptations of Victorian anthropomorphism, for in the seventeenth century Man and his emotional life was kept as distinct from the life of animals as he was from the spirit and associations of landscape. Bewick, born a century and a half later, worked on the edge of a bad period, but he may have been preserved as much by the strictures of wood-engraving as by his own instincts. In the same way Barlow's dry, quiet, unemphatic drawing excludes the violence and false bravura of many Flemish animal pictures. Barlow and Bewick are artists of the same scale and stature, although the one did sometimes attempt very large compositions and the other nothing but tiny ones. Except for the frieze of hounds (Plate 2a), Barlow's big pictures are each an untidy collection of admirable details, almost medieval in their lack of a single focus. He had none of Hondecoeter's assurance and professional skill, and he is at his best, as Vertue recognized, in his drawings and his prints.

If Barlow, then, is the first of his profession in England, he is not the founder of a school, for what follows is not due to his example but to the huge demand for animal pictures which was emerging in his lifetime. Historically at least, a more important event than the whole career of this artist was the publication in 1766 of George Stubbs's *The Anatomy of the Horse.*

Anatomy of the Horse – This work not only reflects great honour on the author, but on the country in which it was produced. France may reap great benefit from the veterinarian school lately established in that country; but what praise is not due to a private person, who, at his own expense, and with the incredible application of years, began, continued, and completed the admirable work before us.

MEDICAL REVIEW, 1767

THIS book with its twenty-four engraved plates and a text by the artist (see also note to Plate 28) was addressed in Stubbs's words 'to those of my own profession and those to whose care and skill the horse is usually entrusted whenever medicine or surgery become necessary to him. I thought it might be a desirable addition to what is usually collected for the study of comparative anatomy, and by no means unacceptable to those gentlemen who delight in horses or keep any considerable number of them. . . . But what I should principally observe to the reader concerning this my performance, is, that all the figures in it are drawn from Nature, for which purpose I dissected a great number of horses; and that, at the same time, I have consulted most of the treatises of reputation on the general subject of anatomy'.

The best previous work of reputation on the anatomy of the horse was that by Carlo Ruini published in 1598, a book which was still being reprinted as late as 1769, for all the other important treatises on this subject before Stubbs's – Snape's *The Anatomy of an Horse* (1683) or *La Parfaite Connoissance des Chevaux* (1734) by J. and G. de Saunier, for example – were plagiarisms of Ruini's observations, theories and illustrations, often made without acknowledgment. In his *History of Veterinary Literature*, Sir Frederick Smith wrote that 'at the hands of Ruini, the subject of equine anatomy jumped at a single bound from the blackest ignorance to relative perfection, the degree of which it is difficult to exaggerate'. Ruini's illustrations are stylish, coherent and alive, and the influence upon seventeenth-century painters of those plates which show the superficial muscles of the animal is easily recognizable, but they remain essentially schematic and inexact. Stubbs did not take the next step forward from Ruini so much as use existing knowledge as the spring-board for a long jump.

The most expert witness for his advance in skill of dissection as well as in observation and descriptive analysis, is one of the leading anatomists of that time, Petrus Camper. In a letter to Stubbs he wrote, 'Sir – If ever I was surprised to see a performance, I was it surely, when I saw yours on the Anatomy of the Horse. The myology-neurology, and angiology of men have not been carried to such perfection in two ages, as these horses by you. How is it possible a single man can execute such a plan with so much accuracy and industry. . . . You will be curious to be acquainted with a Dutchman who admire with so much ecstasy your tables. I am public professor of Medicine, Anat., and Surgery at Groningen. . . . I am sure my acquaintance can be of little use to you, but yours to me of great consequence.' And in another letter he wrote, 'I am amazed to meet in the same person so great an anatomist, so accurate a painter, and so excellent an engraver.'

At no time since Leonardo had art and science been so fruitfully joined, but Stubbs later regretted that the reputation he gained from the publication of his marvellous book 'threw him', as he is reported to have said, 'into the profession of horse-painting'. It also ensured that after 1766 no capable and intelligent painter lacked the knowledge to make his horses plausibly true to appearances, even if he could not share Stubbs's knowledge of natural and pictorial structure.

Having myself been much in the habit of riding young and violent horses with fox hounds, I am well acquainted with the great difficulty and danger there is in leaping them before they are possessed of this power and knowledge. . . . I rode a mare of this description for two seasons; she was four years old and excessively violent. . . . For the first season I had four or five falls a day upon an average and all in consequence of her violent bucking leaps.

HENRY ALKEN: *Beauties and Defects of the Horse*

THE beginnings of English animal painting at the end of the seventeenth century depended partly upon the development of fox-hunting as the major sport of our countryside. In 1600 hunting the stag was still the most favoured form of the chase, although James I, an enthusiastic sportsman, kept a pack of hounds especially for hunting the fox. By the reign of William III, however, several packs of stag hounds had been replaced by fox hounds, the first of these being the Charlton in Suffolk. The Quorn was established in 1698, the Belvoir in 1740, the Pytchley in 1750. About 1762, the Duke of Beaufort made the change from stag to fox hunting, and by the end of the eighteenth century there were few parts of the country in which the fox was not regularly hunted. As the process of enclosure advanced the number of fences and hedges increased and a superior type of horse was required, so that the breeding of special animals for the chase was almost as important as the evolution of the thoroughbred racehorse. This aspect of agricultural history had some influence upon the general character of the hunting picture. The earlier paintings and prints – those of Barlow, Wootton or Tillemans – do not show horses jumping as frequently as the work of a later artist like Alken who filled his pictures with jumps and jumping mishaps which had become a popular motive in hunting literature. The earliest pictures of the Hunt were made in the spirit of the illustrations to such books as Turbevile's *The Noble Arte of Venerie* or Blome's *The Gentleman's Recreation*, which were modelled on continental works of the same kind. The paintings of Barlow, Wootton, or Tillemans represent a compromise; they are descriptive and local in the way that English patronage demanded, but they are not out of touch with the traditions and conventions of Italian or Flemish hunting pieces of which they give a pleasantly genuine, if provincial, version. Perhaps topographical is a better word than descriptive, as they are in general quite undramatic, without, that is, the element of physical excitement and conflict, for the baroque energy of a Rubens hunt is foreign to these artists. If they worked to some restraint, Wootton and Tillemans were, however, still to some degree artistically independent. Their pictures are probably more satisfying in consequence to those who have never ridden to hounds than all but the best work of later generations. The painters of this early period had not yet been absorbed, in fact, by the world of the hunting field and overwhelmed by that complex of custom, law, and expertise which accumulated with the passing of the years. After the middle of the century and with the arrival of the golden age of the sport, the period of Warde, Beckford, Meynell, Nimrod, and Surtees, of Loraine Smith, Squire Osbaldeston, and Mytton, the sporting artist had to be an informed specialist if he was to follow the orders of clients quick to notice the smallest inaccuracy. That may be one reason why Stubbs, a very independent man, painted so few hunting pictures in the last forty years of his life.

Artists were employed to record the history and topography of the sport, its famous runs, incidents, and personalities. A typical example, and a famous one, is the picture by Sawrey Gilpin called *The Death of the Fox*, of which he made several versions and whose subject and treatment influenced many painters, including Ben Marshall. It shows a fox cornered by half-a-dozen hounds in a gully at the edge of a wood. Beyond the trees the huntsmen are coming in for the kill. The picture was made for a wild Yorkshire sportsman, Colonel Thomas

Thornton, who wagered some friends that every February for eleven successive years he would find a Yorkshire fox that would run twenty miles. After the first of them had run for twenty-three miles, the bet was cancelled and Gilpin was commissioned to paint the climax of the chase. The picture had a new violence and realism. Its weakness – one shared by most English hunting pictures – is Gilpin's failure to combine the movements of riders and animals into a single, rhythmical statement of activity. In fact, the best pictures of the hunt were those inspired by the Meet or some moment of repose rather than the Chase or the Death; and even in them the ruthless demand for one kind of accuracy, together with the great difficulties of the subject, often defeated painters who had slight artistic personalities. One instance of this is John Ferneley's famous picture, *The Quorn at Quenby in 1823*, in which every rider, horse, and hound is a portrait. Forty-five pink coats and more, forty-five top-hats, form a monotonous and insignificant pattern, but the painter's ingenuity in making every figure clear and recognizable must have satisfied his patrons. (For this picture twenty members of the hunt subscribed a hundred guineas each, its ownership being then decided by the casting of dice.)

James Ward and Ben Marshall did consistently master the problems: Ward in *Coursing in Sussex*, in *Ralph John Lambton and his Hounds*, and in *John Levett hunting in the Park at Wychnor*; Marshall in *Lord Sondes and his brothers with the Pytchley Hounds*, in *Francis Dukinfield Astley and his Harriers*, in the picture of William Fermor reproduced here (Plate 46) and several other fine works. Marshall was the only painter employed in the hunting field who habitually went beyond the limits of topography and documentation to give his patrons an enduring work of art. If he is the best interpreter of hunting, then Henry Alken is its most typical laureate. Alken was a very prolific recorder of all the sports of the time, racing, shooting, fishing, cockfighting, bull- and badger-baiting, with a journalist's skill for meeting the needs of his public and accepting the limits of their appreciation, which were, indeed, the limitations of his own. In his drawings and prints he offered the humours of the sport – *The Miseries of Hunting*, *Qualified Horses and Unqualified Riders*, *Some Do and Some Do Not – It is all a Notion* – the familiar incidents which could provoke argument and reminiscence – *Dead Beat*, *Gone Away*, *The Death* – and records of famous hunts and famous runs. He was himself a member of the Melton Hunt and, as his book *The Beauties and the Defects in the Figure of the Horse comparatively delineated* shows, he had all the knowledge of hunters and the hunting field to ensure the respect and loyalty of his fellow sportsmen. But he has not much stature or robustness, not much more than a slight, nervous energy; he could not catch the monstrous vitality of Mytton nor match the headlong genius of Jorrocks. His best designs, however, suggest the plain, nimble melody and shapeliness of Egerton Warburton's hunting songs.

> The dew-drop is clinging
> To whin-bush and brake,
> The skylark is singing
> Merrie hunters awake.
> Home to the cover
> Deserted by night
> The little Red Rover
> Is bending his flight.

His neat but slender little figures seldom escape from convention and his handwriting could not suffer much in the process of reproduction; his work states the level of the general requirement. In recording the follies and delights of the chase he never approaches the exuberant humanity of Rowlandson, whose vision found the whole of daily life and not just the smaller world of sport. His point of view is not so sympathetic or his drawings so fluent and engaged as that of less favoured artists like John Leech and Hablot K. Browne.

The greatest of English hunting pictures – Stubbs's *Grosvenor Staghunt* of 1769 – lies between the picturesque conventions of earlier painters and the disorderly naturalism of Alken. The stag has been run to ground by a stream at the foot of a huge oak tree which embraces the figures like a half-open hand. The stream divides the canvas and on the near bank, filling the left-hand corner of the canvas's long rectangle, a huntsman on a grey horse is blowing his horn. The others are sited on the further bank in the order of a frieze, most minutely articulated in their contrasts of movement and repose. Between the two flows a current of thirty hounds, their bodies united and divided with a marvellous control. The picture is too large and complex to be reproduced upon the scale of this book or to be communicated by word, but it is a work which can support the most detailed attention.

Thursday morning arrived, a day of extraordinary excitement and interest to all sportsmen and to millions of others in every part of England from the manufacturer of twelve stories high, to the Yorkshire ploughman; from the Cockney behind his counter, down to the cellarman at Hatchett's; and after all there was very little difference between this and former years, except that the art of cramming horses down people's throats had been practised more successfully than ever was known.

BEN MARSHALL on Derby Day, 1830

HORSE racing and its supporters offered the artist the same opportunities as the hunting field and imposed the same limitations. The earliest racing picture is Barlow's print published in 1687, which shows Charles II, at Dorset Ferry near Windsor Castle, watching the last race meeting he was to attend. The sport did not originate with his enthusiasm, for James I added an interest in racing to his passion for hunting and one of the founders of the English thoroughbred strain,

Thomas Gainsborough: White Dogs: Pomeranian Bitch and Puppy. *Tate Gallery*

the Markham Arabian which came into England in 1617, was probably imported by him to improve the breed of racing horses. It was, however, during Charles's reign that the character and the conditions of the sport were established. Newmarket became his favourite resort and Evelyn's diary for July 1671 characterizes the place in a few words. 'We went to see the stables and fine horses, of which many were kept here at vast expense, with all the art and tendernesse imaginable . . . we returned over Newmarket Heathe, the way being mostly a sweet turf and down, like Salisbury Plaine, the jockeys breathing their fine barbs and racers, and giving them their heates.' Charles instituted a Spring and Autumn meeting there and established the Royal Plates. This is not the place for a detailed account of racing history, but certain events should be mentioned. In 1689, 1704, and 1730 – i.e., during the lifetime of Wootton and Seymour – were imported the three great sires, the Byerley Turk, the Darley Arabian, the Godolphin Arabian, and it was through their noblest descendants Herod (born 1758), Eclipse (born 1764), Matchem (born 1748) that all our finest bloodstock has come. In 1727 appeared the first racing Calendar, Cheney's *An Historical List of All Horse Matches and of all Plates and Prizes run for in England and Wales (of the value of £10 and upwards)*. In 1750 the Jockey Club was founded, and within the next twenty-five years it proved its position as the ruling body of the Turf by instituting a system of racing colours, making laws for the regulation of betting and other measures, etc. In 1773 came the first volume of the *Racing Calendar* and in the year 1778 the St Leger, in 1779 the Oaks, and in 1780 the Derby were run for the first time – i.e. during the most productive period of Stubbs's career.

Of the sport in all its phases, from the training gallop to the rub-down after the race, relatively few accounts have more than a documentary or picturesque value. Until 1872 when the cameras of Muybridge, the American photographer, began to discover the secret of animal gait – the trot, the canter, and the gallop – painters were restricted to conventions for movement which are visually monotonous unless they are controlled by a most distinguished sense of design. From the standpoint of the sportsmen who commissioned racing pictures or bought racing prints, a view of the race from the front or even from an oblique angle was unsatisfactory, for that point of vision sacrificed information to drama; and the attendant problems of structure and perspective were beyond the capabilities of most of the painters employed. And the intervals determined by the facts of a particular race could hardly be neglected. These conditions produced a mass of pictures dominated by a procession of straddled legs, fore legs aloft, hind hooves toeing the turf. No English painter seems to have represented the sport as a physical and emotional contest, the most complicated struggle between men and animals. For that the English racecourse had to await the visit to this country of the French artist, Géricault, whose pictures of jockeys galloping their horses (particularly those at Bayonne and in the Louvre) revive that Baroque dynamism which would seem to be a most appropriate language for expressing the character of the horse-race. Géricault, however, although an enthusiastic horseman, was outside the racing world and, as in the case of the hunting picture, the customs of racing and its strict conditions eventually came to demand a special type of painting, one which lies outside the main stylistic developments of European art.

The best pictures inspired by the Turf are those showing scenes incidental to the race, and many of these are essentially horse portraits with the racecourse as a setting. The distant crowd, the characteristic landscape of the courses with their plain, thick-set buildings, the white rails and posts (which only Stubbs and Marshall used with imagination), the saddles, cloths, and harness, the neat professional movements of the jockeys, the grooms, and stable lads, these offered the best motives for the painter. The master of such sights was Ben Marshall.

There is no evidence beyond his pictures that Stubbs was a sportsman, a racegoer or a hunting man, but Marshall was an expert in the practices and the jargon of the Turf. For more than a third of his working life – from 1812 to 1825 – he lived at Newmarket. He was a sporting journalist whose reports on racing, generally written under the pseudonym Observator, appeared side by side with Nimrod's hunting articles in the *Sporting Magazine*, and his racing pictures show the same alert, imaginative sympathy with the subject which we find in his paintings of the hunting field. His knowledge of these sports and his readiness to provide what his patrons wanted were refined by a remarkable sense of occasion and of the informal drama of the Course and the Field. He is one of the few painters of his kind who have a proper, warm enjoyment of human and animal behaviour, and his work shows a very real appreciation of light and weather. His pictures are clear and active, but they do lack distinction in their drawing, in their statement of form and in the manipulation of paint. Marshall, if not so urgently as Stubbs, needs to be reconsidered beyond the limitations of sporting art; he is a more valuable artist than many of those painters of landscape or history whose romanticism has made them currently fashionable.

Among other painters, not elsewhere mentioned, who made pictures of hunting and racing are John Boultbee (1753–1812), Dean Wolstenholme, snr. (1757–1837), Charles Towne (1763–1840), Samuel Howitt (1765–1822), James Pollard (1772–1867), Abraham Cooper (1787–1868), David Dalby (1790–1840).

THE progress of racing and hunting was certainly the main cause for the development of the horse and dog portrait during the eighteenth century, but by no means all the animal portraits of the time were of race horses, hunters, or fox hounds. The phrases 'favourite horse' or 'favourite dog' which occur frequently in exhibition catalogues show a more traditional reason for animal portraiture. Among such paintings of pets in English art is that, by an unknown artist, of the dog Bungey which belonged to Sir John Harington (Plate 1), Stubbs's picture of Mouton, a Dutch barge dog owned by the first Earl Spencer, who so valued his pet that he once drew his sword to protect it from an interfering passer-by in Piccadilly. And there is Charles Towne's portrait of Old Billy, a horse who died in 1822 at the age of sixty-three. Gainsborough's dog portraits are all of this kind, but horses – thoroughbreds and hunters – were the most common subjects. Their owners required a record of them to accompany the portraits of their family and the views of their estate, perhaps the earliest, apart from Van Dyck's studies of Charles I's horses, being the pictures which Abraham van Diepenbeck made for the first Duke of Newcastle (Plate 7). As the interest in racing spread to all classes many who owned no horses, as well as those who did, liked to have some memorial of the great heroes of the Turf, past and present. Portraits of the Godolphin Arabian, Flying Childers, Eclipse, and other famous animals were multiplied by replicas or copies and through engraving as constantly as the images of a Washington or a Napoleon. In 1790, for example, Stubbs was employed by unknown patrons to make a series of portraits commemorating the most notable animals from the Godolphin Arabian to the best horses of the moment. These were to be exhibited, engraved by his son George Townley Stubbs and published with a historical and descriptive text. The enterprise failed for lack of money, and only sixteen pictures with their engravings were completed. In 1825, Ward published a set of fourteen lithographs of celebrated horses, including Adonis, the favourite charger of George IV, and Copenhagen, and Marengo, the animals ridden at Waterloo by Wellington and Napoleon. And periodicals such as *The Sporting Magazine* regularly used horse portraits for illustrations.

To understand the strict demands which the animal painter had to serve, one has only to read in Sir Theodore Cook's *A History of the English Turf*, a modern echo of the eighteenth-century attitude. 'I am tempted to desire,' he writes, 'that photography had been invented, say, a couple of centuries before Daguerre; for it is a strange fact that even when a really capable artist, who has demonstrated his skill in many other ways, has drawn a horse before the eighteenth century, he has somehow omitted the points for which a breeder will eagerly scrutinize his canvas, and has, with a higher feeling for the general impression of his work which is easily excusable, given the idea of a horse as a whole, as he saw it, without any consideration for what some of us might look for in his paintings later on.' Not only Cook and other latter-day enthusiasts, but the men who originally commissioned the works expected the artist to emphasize the points of the animal. The serious painter had to make a compromise between his sensibility and sense of order, and the expert demands and pride of his employer. When Wootton, Seymour, or John Sartorius paint hunting or racing subjects with anonymous horses, their drawing has, within the limits and conventions of their talent, some freedom and confidence. When they painted a particular horse for a patron there was a conflict between their insufficient knowledge of anatomy and the need to characterize the portrait, to display the animal's points and perhaps even to flatter its appearance. The result is a record of the creature which has neither the merits of realism or symbolism.

After the publication of *The Anatomy of the Horse* and the establishment of Stubbs's mature example, horse (and dog) portraiture moves in three directions. One tendency, the direct result of Stubbs's book, is towards the naturalism of Landseer and Herring. In many pictures, in the later work of Ben Marshall, for instance, the bones and muscles, joints and tendons become so obtrusive that the unity of the animal's form, the natural fluency of its movements, are lost; the 'idea of a horse as a whole' has been sacrificed to the sportsman's requirements. Some painters, Boultbee, Towne, Garrard, Abraham Cooper among them, follow Stubbs in their concentration upon solid form, while others like Ferneley tried to ensure an accurately defined surface.

The second tendency, which first appears in the work of Gilpin, is an interest in animal temperament and expression (Plate 35), one element in that romanticism which is considered later in this essay. Finally, after the middle of the eighteenth century, animal painters begin to suggest that idealization of the horse and the dog, to comment upon their dignity, nobility, or spirit, a habit which ends in the excesses of Landseer and other Victorian artists.

The greatest exponent of the animal portrait was George Stubbs, and this is the most appropriate place in which to consider his whole achievement, one which surpasses that of every other painter treated here. In an essay devoted to Uccello in *Vision and Design*, Roger Fry argued that, 'it is one of the curiosities of the psychology of the artist that he is generally trying hard to do something which has nothing to do with what he actually accomplished; that the fundamental quality of his work seems to come out unconsciously as a by-product of his activity.' If Uccello's conscious activity was the study of perspective, Stubbs's was the pursuit of anatomy. Fry's argument is justified to some degree by the unintentional strangeness, the stillness and inscrutability, of many pictures by him, in particular his portraits of wild animals (see Plate 25) and in the illustrations he made for John Burton's *Essay towards a Complete New System of Midwifery* (1751), but his habit of anatomizing nature is also a main explanation of his genius.

He was born within a year or two of Reynolds, but while the one accepted and spread the neo-classical conventions of their generation, the other seems deliberately to have resisted them. He is reported to have said that his reason for going to Italy in 1754 was 'to convince himself that nature was and is always superior to art whether Greek or Roman', whereas in 1750 Reynolds had written from Rome to his patron, Lord Edgcumbe, 'I am now (thanks to your Lordship) at the height of my wishes, in the midst of the greatest works of art the world has produced.' Reynolds's aesthetic, and that of the Academy which he fathered, required that a painter should base both his study and his production upon the work of his most distinguished predecessors, who alone could instruct him in the limitations and the proper use of Nature. According to Josiah Wedgwood, Stubbs advised the students he taught for a short time at a private academy that 'he would have the learner copy nature and not drawings.'

The word Nature bore many meanings in the eighteenth century and should not be casually used, but no variation of meaning can disguise the lonely position which he maintained among his contemporaries. If he was praised, it was for qualities which were unfashionable and therefore little worthy of praise. Fuseli, whose theories were usually as conventional as his personality and behaviour were eccentric, called Stubbs a facsimilist, because his works were short of idealism and effect. But if the experimental and nature-trusting attitude of Stubbs, his belief in 'nature all' and not 'nature methodized', separated him from his professional colleagues, it attached him all the more closely to the experimental, deductive habits of contemporary science – to Joseph Banks, John and William Hunter, Petrus Camper, with whom he was associated.

In fact, for all his unfashionable realism, Stubbs *did* generalize, but he was always directed by the individuality of the object and not by any ideal of form. (He was, however, as I shall suggest, guided by a very exact and scholarly ideal of design). His profound experience of anatomy and his conviction about the value of studying perspective – the first thing he taught his pupils, we are told – enabled him to achieve what has been denied to most of his countrymen, an unfailing control of solid volumes and of open structures in space. His study of anatomy also enabled him to draw the most refined and eloquent contour and to construct with the simplest modulations of tone. The head of a frightened horse (Plate 23) is a fine example of his tense, poised draughtsmanship; his way of generalizing form and of never modelling beyond the limits of the picture surface is marvellously displayed in the *Prancing Horse* (Plate 21).

The robust man of over six feet who could handle the carcases of horses, walk the eighteen miles to Watford before 10 a.m. at the age of seventy and make pictures on a huge scale, could also manage a minute dissection of a chicken or paint with an excellent tenderness a bunch of flowers in a woman's hand and the silken sheen of her dress. The notion that he was a naïve or a workaday painter, by reason of his uncomplicated vision and his plain methods, must seem absurd when one has examined and analysed a number of his pictures. He was, in fact, a most deliberate designer. Of this the best proof is the series of *Brood Mares and Foals* placed in a landscape or against a grey, unfigured background. In these pictures, the intervals, the rhythm of the contours, the interplay of voids and solids, the management of space shows a power, indeed a sophistication of design, unmatched by any other English artist. His ingenuity appears again in his simple horse portraits which were bound, by convention and demand, to be elementary in their form – a horse standing alone or attended by a groom or ridden by a jockey, in an open landscape, on a racecourse or in a stable-yard or paddock. The viewpoint must always be from a flank to reveal the animal's physical characteristics. Stubbs invariably managed to give poise and a positive stability to these few unvarying components and in two pictures he raised the horse portrait to a heroic level. These are the life-size images of *Whistlejacket* prancing and of *Hambletonian* being rubbed down after a race at Newmarket. They are monumental works, not because of their unusual size – Wootton painted horse portraits of this dimen-

James Ward: Horses Surprised by Wolves. *Tate Gallery*

sion also – but because Stubbs has realized so perfectly the pictorial requirements of that scale.

Finally, he gives the most acceptable account of the animal creation. He is dispassionate and yet sympathetic, curious but not superstitious. There is no false addition of nobility, wildness or pathos, and the owner of a picture originally called Hound Coursing a Stag, who has since given to it the Landseerian title, The Monarch o' the Moor, must have a profound misunderstanding of his intentions and his personality.

The Creator did not bestow so much curiosity and workmanship upon his creatures especially to have them slighted or condemned but to be admired by the rational part of the world, to magnify his own power to all the world.

DERHAM quoted in the introduction to *The British Zoology*, 1776

RARE and exotic wild animals had stirred the imagination of Europeans at least since Roman times. They were used in masques and processions, offered as diplomatic presents, matched against one another in spectacular and often grotesque contests – an elephant against a rhinoceros, a bear against a bull. Many courts of the Middle Ages and the Renaissance maintained extensive menageries, among the most famous being those of René of Anjou at Angers, of Marguerite of Austria at Louvain and Malines, and of François I.

With the scientific revolution of the seventeenth century, however, a different attitude to animals began to be joined to the traditional motives of curiosity and awe. The menagerie was transformed from its original picturesque or ceremonial circumstance into something like the modern zoological park, which is not just an entertainment, but also a centre of scientific enquiry. The same period saw the foundation of modern systematic biology. In England appeared John Ray's classifications of plants and animals, the treatises of Edward Tyson on the porpoise, the rattlesnake, the opossum, and the chimpanzee, and this interest in animal anatomy was supported by the foundation of the Royal Society. The fulfilment of this movement came later with the vast anatomical explorations of John Hunter and its climax, in 1776, with the creation of his revolutionary museum devoted to the anatomy and physiology of the whole animal kingdom. And on varying levels of scientific distinction and accuracy came a flow of literature connected with natural history: such books as Gilbert White's *Natural History of Selborne*, Charles Waterton's *Wanderings in South America*, the various publications of Thomas Pennent and Bewick's *A General History of Quadrupeds*. (The illustrations made for all except Bewick's works are outside the range of this essay.) The great voyages of discovery had often meant the accession of unfamiliar creatures, but in the eighteenth century the custom developed of sending scientists and artists on such explorations; Joseph Banks, for example, sailed with Cook to the Pacific in 1769. Outside England there were the cardinal researches of Linnaeus and the publication of his *Systema Naturae*, the slow unfolding of Buffon's *Histoire Naturelle* and in 1817 Cuvier's *Le Règne Animal*. This widespread investigation of the animal creation meant a new employment for the painter – something more systematic and public than the results of the private curiosity of a Dürer or a Pisanello.

The greatest menagerie of the period was that established by Louis XIV at Versailles and preserved with varying attention until 1794, when the few surviving animals were transferred to the Jardin des Plantes in Paris. The Versailles menagerie was used not only as a marvellous entertainment for Louis' guests, who approached it by water in the decorative craft which sailed on the main waterway of the park, but as a centre for serious study, a place to be visited by distinguished naturalists and anatomists. Louis employed the Flemish painter, Niçaise

Bernaerts, a pupil of Snyders, to paint all the animals admitted to the menagerie, and among other artists who worked there were Boel, de Troy, Boucher, Parrocel, Lancret, Van Loo, Audran, and above all Desportes and Oudry, both of whom continued to make records of the outstanding beasts in the collection throughout their careers. Oudry also painted the rhinoceros which was exhibited in Europe between 1747 and 1751, and the history of this animal's progress across the Continent is worth retailing as evidence of the contemporary interest in rare beasts. The creature was brought from India by a Dutch sea captain in 1747, and while on exhibition at Amsterdam it was seen by the anatomists, Albinus and Petrus Camper. Camper made drawings of the animal and it excited Albinus sufficiently to be figured in two of the plates of his *Sceleti et Musculorum Corporis Humani*. It went from Holland to Germany where it was drawn by the Swiss animal painter, J. E. Ridinger, and in June 1748 (in its great cage drawn by twenty horses) it reached Versailles, where Louis XV tried to buy it for his menagerie, but the price – 100,000 *écus* – was too great. By this time the rhinoceros had become so famous that references to it appear in journals and correspondence. From Paris it went, via Lyon, to Venice, where it appeared in the Carnival, was painted by Longhi and thence taken to Verona to be exhibited in the amphitheatre.

The English Royal Menagerie in the Tower was not in the seventeenth or eighteenth centuries as rich as those at Loo or Versailles, but there were other royal menageries at Windsor and Kew, and among English noblemen who kept wild animals were the Duke of Portland, Lord Shelbourne (Stubbs used to draw from the lion which he kept at his villa on Hounslow Heath), and Sir Thomas Child – at Osterley. Travelling menageries also seem to have been less numerous in England than on the continent, but there was at least one permanent show of wild animals in London, belonging to a dealer named Pidcock of Exeter Change, Strand. It was from

Pidcock, if the story is true, that Stubbs bought a dead tiger, which he spent the night in dissecting; and it was there in 1770 that the Indian rhinoceros was exhibited which Stubbs painted for John Hunter (Colour Plate 1). Hunter's private menagerie at Earl's Court was the most representative in the country, and Stubbs's friendship with him and with his brother William would have acquainted him with many uncommon creatures. Besides the rhinoceros (Plate 1), he painted for John Hunter a yak brought from India by Warren Hastings, and an orang-outang with an albino macaque monkey (Plate 26). In William Hunter's collection at Glasgow University are portraits of a nylghau, a moose, and a pygmy antelope. For Joseph Banks he painted a dingo dog and kangaroo, the first to be seen in Europe and both obtained by the scientist on Cook's first voyage. The kangaroo Stubbs would have had to reconstruct from a dead specimen, for the animal, as Banks reports in his journal, eluded their dogs and had to be shot. He painted a zebra presented to Queen Charlotte and, the most magnificent of all his wild animal portraits, a cheetah sent from India by Lord Pigot as a gift for George III (Plate 20). The animal – life size – stands alert with a scarlet hood drawn back over its ears, in the charge of the two turbaned Indian servants who had brought it to England. One is holding the scarlet sash it wears about its belly, while the other is directing its attention to some animal beyond the right-hand limit of the canvas. Other English painters made occasional portraits of wild animals – J. N. Sartorius, Gilpin, Reinagle, Ward, but the most accomplished was the Swiss-born artist, J. L. Agasse, who spent most of his life in England and whose admirable work shows something of Stubbs's solidity and tenderness (Plate 62).

How shall our attention be engaged by a peasant driving a couple of sheep along the highway?

ABBÉ DU BOS: *Reflections*, 1726

THE neo-classicism of the Enlightenment had not encouraged English artists to treat rural life. In the second half of the eighteenth century (in response to the Englishman's discovery of his scenery and the subsequent cult of the Picturesque) it became first an acceptable theme and then a fashionable one. This new interpretation of country life appears in the details of Gainsborough's landscapes, in the market cart, for example, from the landscape with that title and later in the 'fancy' pictures, as Reynolds called them, in which such incidentals were enlarged to form the whole picture. Because he was a countryman whose artistic habits had been changed in becoming a townee and a portrait painter, Gainsborough looked at his cottage families and their surroundings with a sentimental nostalgia. It is only necessary to compare his view with Stubbs's dispassionate and expert description of reapers or haymakers to see how conventional his idea of the country had become.

The theorists of the Picturesque did not fail to bring animals within their system. 'The ass is generally thought to be more picturesque,' wrote Uvedale Price, 'than the horse and among horses, it is the wild and rough forester or the worn-out cart-horse to which that title is applied. The sleek pampered steed with his high arched crest and flowing mane is frequently represented in painting; but his prevailing character, whether there or in reality, is that of beauty. In pursuing the same mode of inquiry with respect to other animals, we find that the Pomeranian and the rough water-dog are more picturesque than the smooth spaniel or the greyhound, the shaggy goat than the sheep: and these last are more so when their fleeces are ragged and worn away in parts, than when they are of equal thickness, or when they have lately been shorn. No animal indeed is so constantly introduced in landscape, as the sheep, but that as I observed before, does not prove superior picturesqueness; and I imagine that besides their innocent character, so suited to pastoral scenes of which they are the natural inhabitants, it arises from them being of a tint at once brilliant and mellow which unites happily with all objects; and also from their producing when in groups, however slightly the detail may be expressed, broader masses of light and shadow than any other animal.' (*Essay on the Picturesque.*)

That passage might have come from an apology for the art of George Morland, the most typical exponent of the Picturesque animal subject. His paintings were made from the same material as the country ballads sung to amuse the Londoner at Vauxhall and Ranelagh. Morland's figures are types, the burly red-faced farmer, the bustling cottage woman, the rosy-cheeked dairymaid, the moon-faced bumpkin and the country lad gone for a soldier; their setting is the cottage door, the stable, or the village inn, and the animal actors are as stereotyped in their character, the rough forester, the cart-horse, the unkempt collie, the humble donkey, the sluggish pig. The vision – a sophisticated vision – and the message – that rural life has an honest, vulgar innocence – became diffuse through constant repetition, while the painter's handwriting grew slack with overwork. If one method of putting paint on canvas, if to give a picture a broken, picturesque surface is a major virtue, as some critics seem to think, then Morland is a considerable artist. The moments of true observation and sensibility which bring reality to his limited world are, however, rare, but excellent in their kind (see Plate 42).

This picturesque and sentimental view of animals in their natural setting was continued in the work of Morland's brother-in-law, James Ward, who painted such pastoral subjects at every period of his career, in the tidy watercolours of Robert Hills (1769–1844) and in the farmyards of J. F. Herring.

Among its descendants were the illustrations of Randolph Caldicott, the animals in shiny children's books up to our own time and the Silly Symphonies of Walt Disney.

The version of the Picturesque given by J. F. Herring, whose horse portraits have already been mentioned, shows a significant difference from Morland's. Herring lived a generation nearer to general industrialism and to its curatives, the National Trust or the Society for the Preservation of Rural England. His farmyards have the required shagginess of thatch and decay, but they are cleaner and more inviting, the animals are neater, the coats of the horses burnished, the duck's plumage iridescent. The country must offer a more respectable contrast to the town.

Nothing would please but Elephants or Giants.

The cattle breeder GEORGE CULLEY
on the animals of his time, 1776

THE eighteenth century saw the first systematic breeding not only of race horses, but of farm animals. This new scientific improvement of livestock was connected with the extension of enclosures and the resulting improvement in fodder crops, an improvement which increased the country's capacity for stock-bearing. At the end of the seventeenth century sheep were kept more for their wool and their manure than for their meat, and as cattle were mainly used for draught, animals with heavy shoulders were desirable. Breeding was begun early in the century by Sir Thomas Gresley of Drakelow, Derbyshire, who owned a herd of cattle selected and reared for their uniformity of shape and colour and for the excellence of their milk. His precedent was followed by a Warwickshire farmer, Webster of Canley, who started with cows from Drakelow, and it was from him in turn that the heifers came to found the herd of the most famous pioneer in stock-breeding, Robert Bakewell of Dishley Grange, Leicestershire, the improver of the old English heavy horse, the Longhorn breed of cattle and the local Leicestershire sheep. Bakewell's farm was widely known and many visitors came to see not only his animals, but his canals and the irrigated meadows on which mowers were fully employed from May to Christmas. The walls of his rooms were hung with the skeletons of his most notable beasts and there were joints of meat on view preserved in pickle, illustrating the desired smallness of bone or thickness of fat.

With the activities of Bakewell and such disciples or successors as John and Robert Fowler, Matthew and George Culley, and Charles and Robert Colling, it became the practise of breeders to hire out to small farmers pedigree bulls, rams, stallions, and boars. The breeders soon realized how useful it would be to advertise their work and their animals; portraits and the prints which could be made from them offered the best form of testimonial, especially among people not accustomed to reading and often not able to do so. The most lively evidence on this new form of patronage may be found in the memoirs of Thomas Bewick.

'It will be readily supposed,' he wrote, 'that, where such exertions were made, and pains taken to breed the best kinds of all domestic animals, jealousy and envy would be excited and contentions arise as to which were the best. . . . I shall notice an instance, as it happened to occur between my two friends Mr Smith of Woodhall and Mr Bailey. The latter, in connexion with his report on Cheviot sheep, had given a bad figure of a ram of that breed. This was construed into a design to lessen the character of Mr Smith's Cheviot sheep, on which, in April 1798, the latter sent for me to draw and engrave the figure of one of his rams, by way of contrasting it with the figure Mr Bailey had given. The colour Mr Smith gave to the business was, not to find fault with Mr Bailey's figure, but to show how much he (Mr Smith) had improved the breed since Mr Bailey had written his report.'

James Ward: Sheep with a Shorn-Fleece. *Coll. Peter Cochrane*

As in all forms of advertisement, truth was secondary and relative, and the livestock painter was, no doubt, frequently called upon to trouble more than his artistic conscience. Again the evidence comes from Bewick. Between 1793 and 1815 the Board of Agriculture commissioned a series of county reports on the condition of English farming, and he was employed by a breeder at Barmpton to make engravings for one of these. 'After I had made my drawings from the fat sheep,' he wrote, 'I soon saw that they were not approved, but that they were to be made like certain paintings shown to me. I observed to my employer that the paintings bore no resemblance to the animals whose figures I had made my drawings from; and that I would not alter mine to suit the paintings that were shown to me; but if it were wished that I should make engravings from these paintings, I had not the slightest objection to do so, and I would also endeavour to make facsimiles of them. This proposal would not do; and my journey, as far as concerned these fat cattle makers, ended in nothing. I objected to put lumps of fat here and there where I could not see it, at least not as exaggerated a way as the painting before me. . . . Many of the animals were, during this rage for fat cattle, fed up to as great a weight and bulk as it was possible for feeding to make them; but this is not enough; they were to be figured monstrously fat before the owners of them could be pleased. Painters were found quite subservient in this guidance, and nothing else would satisfy.'

Such monsters as Bewick mentions, cattle and pigs as well as sheep, were not only painted but exhibited in public, being carried from town to town in wagons; among these were the Lincolnshire Ox painted by Stubbs (Plate 24), the white Shorthorn heifer bred by Robert Colling and painted by Weaver (Plate 57) and Charles Colling's Durham Ox, said to have been without a fault. This animal travelled round England to advertise the improved Shorthorn breed which succeeded the Longhorns, and such famous beasts became as much part of a contemporary mythology as *Eclipse* or the touring rhinoceros of the 1740s.

As the enthusiasm for scientific breeding and indeed for all forms of agricultural progress developed in the decades about the turn of the century, more systematic efforts were made to record the results of livestock improvement. In 1810 George Garrard, a pupil of Sawrey Gilpin and a sculptor as well as a painter who learnt much from Stubbs's example, published with the encouragement of the Board of Agriculture thirty-seven coloured aquatints of *Different Varieties of Oxen common in the British Isles*. The most ambitious of such schemes concerned James Ward. In 1800 he met Sir John Sinclair, President of the Agricultural Society, who employed him to paint a pedigree cow – his first work of this character – and introduced him to others interested in farming, among them Lord Somerville and the Duke of Bedford. Under this powerful patronage, Ward became not only the most popular cattle painter of the moment, but received a commission from the Society and the print firm of Boydell, who provided the money, to paint a series of two hundred portraits of the representative breeds of British cattle, sheep, and pigs. These were to be made to a uniform size and subsequently engraved, the artist to receive fifteen guineas for each subject. In fulfilment of his contract, Ward travelled through Wales, the Welsh border counties, Devon, Cornwall, Somerset, Dorset, Berkshire, and Wiltshire; by 1805 he had finished most of the necessary drawings as well as twenty-five of the paintings. By that date, however, none of the engravings had been published, Boydells were moving towards bankruptcy, and they refused to pay Ward more than the amount he had already received. Between their failure and his uncompromising temperament the project collapsed, although some of the completed panels are the best works to emerge from this unpromising form of patronage.

Among the other artists who painted cattle and other livestock for breeders were Ben Marshall, whose work in this kind included portraits of the Royal cattle at Windsor made for the Prince Regent in 1796, James Barenger, John Boultbee, H. B. Chalon, Abraham Cooper, and Charles Towne. The most famous Victorian cattle painter was T. Sidney Cooper (1805–1895).

I find Mr S. repents much his having established this character for himself [as an animal painter] and wishes to be considered as an history & portrait painter.

WEDGWOOD TO BENTLEY, 1779

PERHAPS the main conflict in the development of English painting before impressionism was that between the standards of connoisseurs or men of taste and the more ambitious artists, on the one hand, and the realities of English patronage, on the other. The belief that history painting was the noblest form of art and one to which all should aspire lasted well into the nineteenth century, but such men of high intention as James Barry and Benjamin Robert Haydon failed for lack of support. Reynolds, the most intelligent and scholarly sponsor of Academic theories, realized that for him and many of his contemporaries some kind of artistic compromise would have to be found between the language of the Grand Manner and the conventions of the portrait, the form which English patrons demanded from native artists.

The same situation troubled animal painters, and with more reason, for their genre came lower in the scale of value than the human portrait. Ward, alone among animal painters, attempted an allegorical subject on a heroic scale and in a manner which made no concession to his common reputation. His labours to fulfil the design which, in 1820, won him the prize offered by the British Institution for a work commemorating Wellington's victory at Waterloo, disrupted his career as disastrously as Barry's efforts at the Society of Arts. Other animal painters found an answer, like Reynolds, in compromise and it is interesting to recall that his ownership of Stubbs's *Phaeton and the Chariot of the Sun* is one of the few connexions between these two artists which can be traced. This painting was an example of what may be called an animal history piece and Stubbs modelled a version of the same subject for Wedgwood. The catalogues of the Royal Academy and of the Incorporated Society of Artists mention other pictures by which he tried to establish a more eminent reputation through this type of work. All represent subjects containing animals (or centaurs at least): *Hercules and Antaeus*, *Nessus and Dejanira*, *The Judgment of Hercules*, and a *Portrait of a Young Lady in the Character of Una from Spenser's Faerie Queen*, with the lion and an ass. That all these had to be put into the sale of his effects suggests that Stubbs had no success in changing his repute, but he was not the only painter to try this kind of compromise. Garrard was another, and Sawrey Gilpin also made some history pieces, the most famous in his lifetime being *The Election of Darius* (Plate 33). In the year of his death he exhibited a picture based upon some lines from the second act of Macbeth called *Duncan's Horses*, which can hardly have differed much from his *Horses frightened in a Thunderstorm*. The fashionable taste for illustrating themes from Shakespeare was already twenty years old, and this must be one of the few passages in the plays which offered the animal painter an easy opportunity. The subject was later used by Ward, and among that artist's history pieces are *Daniel in the Lion's Den* and *The Fall of Phaeton* (Plate 52).

But as the strong curb's courser hears the distant strains
With cymbals harshly clashing, his bounding heart beats high
Th' fiery flood, then hurrying, threeke through all his veins;
Swells in each quivering limb, and glares the vivid eye.
He tares up the ground;
As repeated the sound;
And responds to the cry –

JAMES WARD: from his description
of his *Allegory of Waterloo*

IN 1821 the French painter Géricault brought to London, for exhibition at the Egyptian Hall, his painting, *Le Radeau de la Méduse*. In May of that year he wrote to his friend, Horace Vernet, of the excellence of the contemporary English school as it was presented at the Royal Academy exhibition, and noted particularly '*des animaux peints par Ward et Landseer, agé de dix-huit ans; les maîtres n'ont rien produit de mieux en ce genre*'. Géricault was not the first or the last French artist of the nineteenth century to be excited by English painting; the relationship between Delacroix and Constable is familiar and well documented, but not so widely recognized are the connexions between English and French animal painting, beginning with the career of Carle Vernet, whose pictures of horses were much influenced by English examples. It is, however, the links between Géricault and his English contemporaries which are the most interesting.

There is the letter which has been quoted, the fact that Géricault made copies from prints by Stubbs – one of a tiger, another of a lion attacking a horse. There is the remarkable similarity of style and feeling shared by the anatomy studies of Ward and Géricault as well as by many of their other works. There is the common interest of these artists with Delacroix and others, English and French, in animals frightened, attacking each other or striving in conflict with human figures. In Ward's work occur such themes as a boa-constrictor attacking a horse (Plate 53), bulls fighting, a lion savaging a tiger, stags fighting, a 'Liboya' serpent destroying a tiger, wagon horses frightened by lightning. In the work of Géricault – riders restraining their excited horses, lion hunts, herdsmen rounding up bulls in an enclosure, a stag attacked by dogs; in Delacroix – lion and tiger hunts, Arab horses fighting in a stable, horses frightened by lightning. One source of these similarities is, of course, the revived influence of Rubens. In France the challenge to the classicism of David and his school which came after the defeat of Napoleon involved a return to *Rubénisme*, and the restoration of the Marie de Medici series to the Louvre in 1816 helped to strengthen that painter's hold upon the younger generation. In England the signs of Rubens's influence had appeared earlier – in Constable's work before 1810 and in Ward's in 1804. His *St Donat's Castle; Bulls Fighting*, of that year was a deliberate effort to emulate the *Château de Steen: Autumn*, which he had seen the previous year in the collection of Sir George Beaumont.

Ward and his French contemporaries, however, for all their debt to Rubens, treat hunting and other animal subjects of the kind already mentioned with quite a different purpose and motive. Rubens, Snyders, or Fyt had made their pictures in a period when stag or boar hunting, combats between wild creatures and such perverse amusements as fox-tossing were a favourite entertainment for their patrons. By the early nineteenth century most of these practices had vanished in England and France, and if Rubens designed his animal paintings to give vicarious pleasure to his patrons, Ward, Géricault, or Delacroix painted their similar pictures mainly to please themselves. The horse and wild animals became most important elements in the body of romantic symbolism. They represented the vital principal in Nature and the force of instinct, when reason and the intellect were under suspicion. Hazlitt praised the character of King Lear as 'an example of individual passion. We see,' he wrote, 'the ebb and flow of the feeling, its pauses and feverish starts, its impatience of opposition.' A bridled horse fighting at the curb or a hunted lion presented the same instinctive, unreasoning force and the opposition of restraint. If Keats could think of identifying himself with a bird so that 'if a sparrow comes before my window, I take part in its existence and pick about the gravel', then Ward could find in some wild creature a reflection of his own impulses and frustrations, an outlet for his nervous will to self-expression and self-exploration. The wildest of his wild animal pictures often came at periods of personal contest and disappointment, and it is interesting to recall that after the crisis in Géricault's personal affairs which preceded his visit to Rome in 1817, he found a symbol of his anguish and a relief for his disquiet in the race of wild horses along the Corso, the subject which mainly occupied him during his stay in the city. It is not surprising to find among Ward's writings one pamphlet against the docking of horses' tails and another *In Defence of the Beard*, which begins 'Nature gave the beard' and includes the question, 'What would a lion be without his mane?'

In France, animal painting had to be revived after thirty years of classicism, Carle Vernet being the only important *animalier* between Géricault or Barye and the time of Oudry and Desportes. In England Ward's painting was part of an unbroken succession. There is evidence of pictures by his older contemporaries similar to those now being considered. Philip Reinagle's Academy Diploma picture of 1807 was entitled '*An Eagle and a Vulture disputing with a Hyena*. In the 1790's Northcote exhibited scenes of conflict between a vulture and a snake, a vulture and a lamb, a tiger and a crocodile, and between other creatures. Earlier there had been Gilpin's *Horses frightened in a Thunderstorm* (Plate 31) which hardly project the moment of terror with Delacroix's physical force and reality, but have a true unity of action and mood.

The earliest examples of this kind of subject, with the exception of a few drawings by Barlow, are a sequence of pictures by Stubbs of a horse attacked by a lion, of which the original versions date from the late 1760's (see also note to Plate 22). In the first scene the lion is stalking the horse at a distance; in the second – *A Horse frightened by a Lion* (Plates 22 and 23) – it has closed upon its prey, which now draws back in terror; in the third, the lion is on the horse's back tearing at its crest. The last seems to have been the most popular of the three and was the incident copied by Géricault. There are versions of the picture in oil and enamel colours and they were all engraved, by the painter and by others. It is significant to find that two of the scenes were the works chosen to represent Stubbs in a book published in 1832 at the full tide of English romanticism, Hamilton's *The English School . . . from the days of Hogarth*.

And yet these and other pictures of a similar kind (*Bulls Fighting*, *A Lion devouring a Stag*, and *Stallions Fighting*) are essentially different from those of Ward or Géricault. Fuseli wrote that Stubbs's horses 'depend more on the facsimilist's precision than the painter's spirit', and Haydon considered that 'Stubbs is useful, but his horses are not grand enough. They may be just as correct without violating the principle of effect'. Stubbs, however, was not concerned, in Fuseli's phrase, to 'transpose himself into his subject', but to examine and represent the form of things with the least personal self-expression. If he did, in fact, in Morocco see a lion attacking a horse, he viewed it no doubt with the curiosity of an anatomist. If such a scene by Ward or Delacroix is a revival of the baroque, then Stubbs's version is a denial of all that word suggests; the spectator is not drawn physically or emotionally into a vortex. The lion and the horse are exhibiting rather than experiencing the sensations which their actions imply. They are constructed in the manner of sculpture and composed planimetrically. They inhabit a landscape which does not move in sympathy with their behaviour as it would do in a hunting

William Etty: A Peacock. *Manchester City Art Gallery*

scene by Rubens. It is only necessary to compare these pictures with the very late and gentle baroque animal pictures of Stubbs's contemporary, Ridinger, to prove his classicism.

I have suggested that during the first forty years of the nineteenth century animals acquired a significance, as the vehicles of romantic self-fulfilment, which they had not previously assumed. The same period saw a new association of the human and animal creation which resembles the association between man and natural landscape to be found in the work of Wordsworth and other writers. In fact one of the most typical statements in poetry of the former outlook occurs in a poem by Wordsworth, in his *Hart-leap Well*, which inspired Constable's *Cenotaph*. It describes both the chase of a hart, which only dies from exhaustion after outrunning its pursuers, and the memorial which the leader of the hunt raises to its honour. In the last few stanzas come these lines spoken by the Poet to a shepherd who has shown him the monument:

> This Beast not unobserved by Nature fell;
> His death was mourned by sympathy divine.
>
> The Being that is in the clouds and air,
> That is in the green leaves among the groves
> Maintains a deep and reverential care
> For the unoffending creature whom he loves.

Connected with that idea was an increasing interest in the emotional ties between men and animals. Keats states the attitude in one of his letters. 'The greater part of Men make their way with the same instinctiveness, the same unwandering eye from their purposes, the same animal eagerness as the Hawk. The Hawk wants a Mate, so does the man – look at them both, they set about and procure one in the same manner. I go among the fields and catch a glimpse of a stoat or a field mouse peeping out the withered grass – the creature hath a purpose and its eyes are bright with it.' And he also wrote of

> The man who with a bird,
> Wren or Eagle, finds his way to
> All its instincts.

A similar idea, no doubt, encouraged Ward to entitle one of his pictures *The Council of Horses* and another *L'Amour de Cheval* (Plate 48). An example of how this habit of mind was later exaggerated into absurdity occurs in the work of the Victorian cattle painter, T. Sidney Cooper. Like Ward, he attempted to rival Paul Potter's famous bull. 'It was a single animal standing, being in the centre of the canvas, three-fourths the size of Nature, with a group of cows in the extreme distance and I called the picture *Separated, but not Divorced*.' (*My Life*. T. S. Cooper.)

The same interest was expressed in other forms. In 1820 H. B. Chalon published a group of lithographs devoted to the expression of certain emotions in horses, and in 1841, Ward made a series of paintings describing the actions and emotions of the horse, including scenes displaying disappointment, fear, self-possession, depression, etc. A favourite stage turn of the time was a dying horse who also appeared in a drama called *Timour the Tartar*, in which it performed a number of tricks including dancing, fighting, and scrambling up a precipice. This is appropriate for a final word about James Ward whose name has appeared so frequently in this essay. At his worst he could be a slave to the conventions of the Picturesque; too often he indulged to excess his sentiment, his passion for the grandiose and the sensational; he was a victim of the mannerism of his great technical fluency. In his tremendous output, however, there are many paintings and innumerable drawings which justify Géricault's enthusiasm if not his comparison with the past, and they invite a proper study and selection of his work.

Ward and Landseer – Géricault's association of these names was correct, for Ward's painting was on the brink of the Victorian decline.

In representing beasts, man has to think of them essentially with their skins on and with their souls in them. He is to know how they are spotted, wrinkled, furred and feathered; and what the look of them is in the eyes; and what grasp, or cling, or trot, or pat, in their paws or claws. . . . He is to take every sort of view of them in fact except one, the Butcher's view . . . the knowledge of bones and meat, of joint and muscle is more a hindrance than a help.

RUSKIN: *The Eagle's Nest*

LANDSEER resembled Millais, for both were precociously talented and both, before falling to the temptations of their age, painted some admirable pictures. It is fair to remember also, that the worst of Landseer's pictures are more capably made and no more degraded in their sentiment than a host of animal pictures exhibited after 1850. A painting such as *The Old Shepherd's Chief Mourner* exaggerates very little the view of Ruskin (who said of Landseer that 'it was not by a study of Raphael that he attained his eminent success, but by a healthy love of Scotch terriers') that 'there is in every animal's eye a dim image and gleam of humanity, a flash of strange light through which their life looks out and up to our great mystery of command over them and claims the fellowship of the creature if not of the soul' (*Academy Notes, 1858*). Or again ' . . . there are few birds or beasts that have not a range of character, which if not equal to that of the horse or dog, is yet as interesting within narrow limits, and often in grotesqueness, intensity or wild and timid pathos, more singular and mysterious' (*Lectures on Art, 1870*).

There is something of that quest for animal character,

refined by the presence of satire, in the margins of some paintings by Hogarth (Plates 10, 11). When, in 1859, members of the original Pre-Raphaelite Brotherhood formed a new association of those who had shared or supported their convictions, they called it the Hogarth Club, thereby acknowledging the link between such works as Holman Hunt's *The Awakened Conscience* or Rossetti's *Found*, and the serious intention of Hogarth's 'modern, moral subjects'. And as some of the best animal painting of the eighteenth century may be discovered in the latter's work as significant additions to the main design, so some of the best Victorian animals can be found concealed in Pre-Raphaelite pictures – the lambs in Millais's *Pretty Baa Lambs*, the dogs in Madox Brown's *Work*, the puppy playing in the foreground of Brett's *Stonebreaker*, the cat in *The Awakened Conscience*, and the lamb in *The Hireling Shepherd* (Plate 64).

NOTES ON THE ARTISTS AND PAINTINGS

The artists are arranged alphabetically. Sizes are given in inches, height first, except in certain cases where it has not been possible to discover the dimensions or the present owner of the work. The notes which follow the entries are not intended to give the detailed information provided by a conventional catalogue raisonné, *but rather to amplify a necessarily brief text. (Biographical notes have only been provided for those artists whose main work was animal painting or who are little known.)*

J. L. AGASSE (1780–1849). This artist was a Swiss, born in Geneva. After working under David and Horace Vernet in Paris, where he also studied at the Veterinary College, he came to London in 1805 and remained in England (where he died), for the greater part of his life. He exhibited at the Royal Academy and acquired a great reputation, devoting himself to all the customary themes of English animal painting, the horse portrait, portraits of wild animals, scenes of the fox-hunt and the horse-race, the meet, the market, and the stable-yard.

The Nubian Giraffe. Oil on canvas. 50 × 40. Signed. Reproduced by gracious permission of Her Majesty the Queen.

This animal was presented by Mohammed Ali Pasha of Egypt to George IV in 1827 and was probably the first of its kind to be seen in England. It was sent here in charge of the two attendants seen in the picture. [PLATE 62]

HENRY ALKEN (1785–1841). Henry Thomas Alken was the most famous member of four generations of artists, his grandfather being a carver, his father an architect and engraver, two of his brothers and two of his sons sporting artists. He made many drawings and etchings not only of British and foreign sports, but also of the customs and manners of his time. His publications include *The Beauties and Defects in the Figure of the Horse comparatively delineated* (1816), *Sporting Sketches* (1817), *National Sports of Great Britain* (1820).

The Melton Hunt, 1826: Getting Away. Pencil on paper. Coll. unknown.

This was one of a set of drawings commissioned by John Murray to illustrate Nimrod's *The Chase, the Road, and the Turf.* [PLATE 60]

ANON (*c.* 1600).

Portrait of Sir John Harington's Dog, Bungey (or Bungy). Oil on canvas. 29 × 34½. Coll. Lord Fairhaven.

This is probably the earliest extant animal portrait in English art. A portrait of Bungey, a large spaniel, also appears on the decorated title page of Harington's translation of Ariosto's *Orlando Furioso*. On a scroll issuing from the dog's mouth are the words *fin che vegna*, the motto of Olivero, a character in the poem, whose device is a crouching spaniel. An account of Bungey's many excellences is given in a letter from Harington to Prince Henry dated 14 June 1608. As this picture had clearly been painted by that time, it can be dated about 1600.

[PLATE 1]

FRANCIS BARLOW (*c.* 1626–1702). According to Vertue, Barlow was born in Lincolnshire and on coming to London became a pupil of 'W. Shepherd a face-painter'. His surviving pictures are mainly large decorative pieces devoted to animals and game. He was a prolific draughtsman and many of his drawings were engraved either by himself, by Hollar and Place, or by less capable artists such as Soly and Dudley. Among other works he made designs for *Æsop's Fables* (1665), *Several Ways of Hunting, Hawking, and Fishing according to the English Manner* (1671), and for *Divers Species of Birds*. Barlow also designed General Monk's funeral hearse and made drawings of the funeral, which were engraved by R. White.

Hare and Hounds (detail). Oil on canvas. Height 50 in. Coll. Lord Onslow.

This is one of the six paintings made for Denzil Onslow, the hounds represented being those known at the time as Southern-mouthed Hounds. A breeding of these animals with the lighter and faster Northern hound – with the addition of greyhound stock – probably produced the modern foxhound. [PLATE 2a]

Hare-hunting. Pen and wash. 21 × 31. Coll. Ashmolean Museum, Oxford.

This drawing, which includes a part of the painting reproduced in Plate 2a, was subsequently engraved by Hollar. [PLATE 2b]

Fish. Oil on canvas. Coll. unknown.

Attributed to Barlow. This type of subject was to become even more popular in the nineteenth century. [PLATE 3]

Cat and Kittens. Pen and wash. 5 × 7¼. Dated 1684. Witt Collection, Courtauld Institute.

It was not until the nineteenth century that portraits of cats became common. Before the modern interest in the animal as a pet which first became widespread in France, the cat was more frequently depicted unsympathetically as a savage and predatory creature, associated with magic and evil. [PLATE 4]

The Decoy at Pyrford at Sunset with Waterfowl startled by a Bird of Prey. Oil on canvas. 108 × 159. Coll. Lord Onslow.

Another of the pictures Barlow painted for Denzil Onslow. Shaw Sparrow has suggested that it represents a part of the decoy at Onslow's house at Pyrford, mentioned in the diary of his friend John Evelyn. [PLATE 5]

Elephant and Rhinoceros. Pen and wash. 21 × 30. Witt Collection. Courtauld Institute.

This subject, not uncommon at the period, derives from a passage in Pliny's Natural History describing the hostility supposed to exist between the elephant and the rhinoceros, a passage which inspired not only pictures of the contest but various attempts to arrange a battle involving the two creatures. Barlow has derived his drawing from earlier sources, the rhinoceros being one of many re-interpretations of Dürer's portrait of 1515. It was probably taken from one of the later versions, perhaps from Gessner or Johnston, rather than from Dürer's print. (For a detailed account of the influence of Dürer's rhinoceros, see Professor F. J. Cole's 'Dürer's Rhinoceros in Zoological Literature' in *Science, Medicine, and History*, O.U.P., 1954.) An Indian rhinoceros was exhibited in London during Barlow's lifetime, in 1685. [PLATE 6]

THOMAS BEWICK (1753–1828). Born near Newcastle, where he spent most of his life. At the age of fourteen he was apprenticed to an engraver on metal, Ralph Beilby, but he devoted most of his time to wood engraving and in 1775 he received a prize from the Society of Arts for five cuts illustrating Gay's *Fables.* After a period away from Newcastle, in London and elsewhere, he took up partnership with Beilby in 1777. His best work is to be found in *The Select Fables* (1784), his *General History of Quadrupeds* (1790), and his *History of British Birds* in two volumes (1797 and 1804). His memoir of his life appeared posthumously.

A Starling. Watercolour. $7\frac{7}{8} \times 10\frac{1}{16}$. Witt Collection, Courtauld Institute.

Bewick made the engravings for many of the illustrations to his *History of Birds* and a few of the *Quadrupeds* from watercolours like the one reproduced here. [PLATE 39]

LUKE CLENNELL (1781–1840). The son of a farmer, Clennell was apprenticed to Thomas Bewick from 1797 until 1804. He gave up engraving for painting about 1810 and during the next seven years painted a great variety of subjects, his most famous works being *The Waterloo Charge* and *The Banquet of Allied Sovereigns in the Guildhall.* In 1817 he lost his reason.

Baggage Waggons in a Storm. Oil on canvas. Coll. unknown. [PLATE 58]

CHARLES COLLINS (d. 1744). Little is known of this artist, who was a painter of animals and birds. In 1736 a set of twelve prints of British birds after his drawings was engraved by Fletcher and Mynde.

A Red-throated Diver. Pen and watercolour. $14\frac{3}{4} \times 21\frac{1}{8}$. Witt Collection, Courtauld Institute. [PLATE 12]

MARMADUKE CRADOCK (*c.* 1660–1717). Born at Somerton in Somerset. On coming to London he was apprenticed to a decorative painter, whose trade he himself followed. Cradock painted in the manner of Barlow and was, according to Vertue, 'one of the best painters of birds and beasts of all his contemporaries.' A number of his bird groups were engraved by Sympson between 1740 and 1743.

Fighting Cock, four years old, belonging to Baron Hollis. Oil on canvas. $32 \times 27\frac{1}{2}$. Coll. unknown.

This picture was attributed to Cradock when shown at the Country Life in British Art Exhibition (1934). It shows a cock growing its plumage after its career had ended. The canvas is inscribed with the following lines:

This is the Duckwing, beat him if you can
That once disappointed a possetive man
Mr Oldham by name and his famous red dun
Were in ninety four brushes, beaten sure as a gun.
It was a very odd thing and a strange disaster
That the Red dun should so deceive his Master
Some Cocker, cry'd out, who were then in ye pit,
Who in Detts name could have ere thought it
So his picture now drawn the feat to remember
And the Cock too hereafter, when we are to Ye end of Dec.

L. A. Jan. 26th, 1696. [PLATE 8]

ABRAHAM VAN DIEPENBECK (1596–1675). A Flemish artist, a pupil of Rubens, who was employed by William Cavendish, Duke of Newcastle, probably about 1629, to paint portraits of his horses and

George Stubbs: Mares and Foals in a Landscape. *National Trust (Ascott Collection)*

also to provide the illustrations for his famous book, *A New Method to Dress Horses* (1657).

One of the Duke of Newcastle's Horses, with a View of Welbeck. Oil on canvas. 78 × 90½. Coll. Duke of Portland.

This picture by a foreign artist, one of twelve which were made for the Duke of Newcastle, is included here as they were probably the earliest horse portraits of their kind to be painted in England. They must have been well known to Wootton and to Stubbs who painted at Welbeck. [PLATE 7]

WILLIAM ETTY (1787–1849).

A Peacock. 22½ × 31½. Oil on canvas. Coll. Manchester City Art Gallery.

This painting is, perhaps, a study for the peacock in the large *Judgement of Paris* exhibited at the R.A. in 1826 and now in the Lady Lever Gallery, Port Sunlight. [PLATE V, FACING P. 48]

JOHN FERNELEY (1782–1860). The son of a Leicestershire wheelwright, Ferneley was first apprenticed in that trade and then in 1803 sent to London to study painting under Ben Marshall. In 1806 he gained his first important commission, being employed by Assheton Smith, who had just purchased the Quorn Hounds. In 1814 he established himself at Melton Mowbray, where he lived and worked for the rest of his life, gaining a great reputation as a painter of horse portraits and hunting subjects. Two of his children, John and Claud Loraine, followed his profession.

Portrait of a Hunter. Oil on panel. 5¾ × 9½. Coll. Sidney F. Sabin.

This picture, which dates from 1841, was selected by Ferneley as his idea of 'a good portrait of a modern hunter' to embellish a book called *The Horse* by Nimrod, intended to be the standard work on the subject. [PLATE 59]

THOMAS GAINSBOROUGH (1727–88).

White Dogs: Pomeranian Bitch and Puppy. Oil on canvas. 32¾ × 44. Coll. Tate Gallery. (Reproduced by courtesy of the Trustees.)

Gainsborough painted several dog portraits, but none of these were exhibited during his life time. [PLATE II, FACING P. 25]

Portrait of a Dog, Bumper. Oil on canvas. 13¾ × 11¼. Coll. Sir Edmund Bacon.

The canvas bears this inscription:

Thos. Gainsborough Pinxit Anno 1745
Bumper A most remarkable sagacious Cur. [PLATE 29]

Study of an Old Horse. Oil on canvas. 21¾ × 25½. Coll. Tate Gallery. (Reproduced by courtesy of the Trustees.)

Whether this painting was a study for a particular picture is not known, but this very Picturesque horse would have made a suitable inhabitant for any of Gainsborough's later pastoral or 'fancy' pictures. [PLATE 30]

SAWREY GILPIN (1733–1807). Born at Carlisle, the son of an amateur artist, he became in 1749 a pupil of the marine painter, Samuel Scott. Among his early patrons was the Duke of Cumberland, at whose stud Gilpin seems to have acquired his knowledge of horses. He became President of the Incorporated Society of Artists in 1774 and was elected R.A. in 1797. He made portraits of domestic and wild animals, hunting scenes (including his famous and influential *The Death of the Fox*) and a number of history pictures. He worked with George Barret the elder, Farington, and Zoffany. His brother was the Reverend William Gilpin, author of many books of travel in search of the Picturesque.

Horses frightened in a Thunderstorm. Oil on canvas. 33 × 49. Coll. Royal Academy of Arts.

Gilpin made a number of versions of the subject, this being presented as his Diploma work on becoming a Royal Academician in 1797. Such a picture may be compared with works devoted to a similar theme by Géricault and Delacroix, but there is no reason to suppose that the French artists knew of this or other examples. [PLATE 31]

Gulliver describing Fortification to the Horses. 48 × 62. Coll. York Art Gallery.

Between 1768 and 1772 Gilpin exhibited three pictures at the Society of Artists illustrating Gulliver's voyage to the country of the Houyhnhnms. A fourth picture, the one reproduced here, was exhibited at the British Institution in 1808 and shows the incident from Chapter 5 in which Gulliver explains the nature of war. [PLATE 32]

The Election of Darius. Oil on canvas. 78 × 106¾. Coll. York Art Gallery.

This was the most ambitious of Gilpin's occasional essays in history painting and the Grand Manner. The subject is taken from the chapters in the Thalia of Herodotus which describe how Darius was chosen from six claimants to be king of Persia. The crown was to be given to the one whose horse neighed first after sunrise on a certain day. The groom of Darius, seen in the picture leading his master's animal, ensured his election by tethering close at hand a mare whom the horse had already covered. [PLATE 33]

Bears. Pen and wash. 7½×11. Witt Collection, Courtauld Institute. [PLATE 34]

A Grey Arab Horse. Oil on canvas. 27¾×35½. Coll. Fitzwilliam Museum, Cambridge. [PLATE 35]

JOHN FREDERICK HERRING (1795–1865). It is said that Herring was prompted to become an animal painter by seeing the St Leger run at Doncaster in 1814. He worked first as a coach painter and then became a coach driver. He had no training as an artist except for a short period with Abraham Cooper. He painted a great number of horse portraits and was also well known for his farmyard scenes and hunting pictures. His three sons were also painters.

White Horse outside a Cottage. Oil on canvas. 30×25. Private Collection. [PLATE 61]

WILLIAM HOGARTH (1697–1764).

The Painter and his Pug. Oil on canvas. 35½×27½. Coll. Tate Gallery. (Reproduced by courtesy of the Trustees.) Signed and dated 1745.

The animal in this portrait is Hogarth's favourite dog, Trump, which was also modelled by the sculptor, Roubiliac. [PLATE 9]

A Cat – detail from *The Graham Children*. Dated 1742. Detail 6 in. long. Coll. Tate Gallery (Reproduced by courtesy of the Trustees.)

The cat, which is climbing over the back of a chair, has been attracted by a goldfinch in a cage. [PLATE 10]

Detail from '*A Rake's Progress*', *Scene V*. *c*. 1733. Detail 6 in. long. Coll. Sir John Soane's Museum.

This is an excellent example of Hogarth's frequent use of animals, either to provide an ironic comment upon the behaviour of human figures or to give an accent of movement or verisimilitude to the composition. The fifth scene of this series depicts the Rake's marriage to an elderly heiress. [PLATE 11]

WILLIAM HOLMAN HUNT (1827–1910).

Detail from *The Hireling Shepherd*. Dated 1851. Detail 12 in. long. Coll. Manchester City Art Gallery.

Holman Hunt explained the symbolism of his picture as follows: The shepherd is a type of the 'muddle-headed pastors who instead of performing services to their flock – which is in constant peril – discuss vain questions of no value to any human soul. My fool has found a Death's Head Moth, and this fills his little mind with forebodings of evil, and he takes it to an equally sage counsellor for her opinion. . . . While she feeds her lamb with sour apples, his sheep have burst bounds and got into the corn.' [PLATE 64]

SIR EDWIN LANDSEER (1802–73). Son of an engraver, John Landseer. At the age of eleven he won the silver palette of the Society of Arts for animal drawing and two years later exhibited for the first time at the Royal Academy. In 1824 he paid a visit to the Highlands of Scotland, a journey which was to have a great influence upon the course of his painting. He was elected A.R.A. in 1826 and R.A. in 1831, and was knighted in 1850. Landseer's work, besides being the most popular of his time, was also greatly admired by Queen Victoria and Prince Albert, both of whom he instructed in drawing and etching. In addition to being a painter, mainly of portraits and a wide variety of animal subjects, comic, sentimental and romantic, he was a sculptor whose most famous achievement was the lions at the base of Nelson's Column.

The Hunting of Chevy Chase. Oil on canvas. 55½×67. Coll. National Art Collections Fund.

The fifteenth-century Border ballad *Chevy Chase* tells of the rivalry of Percy and Douglas, of how Earl Percy of Northumberland vowed to hunt for three days across the Scottish border and of the battle which ensued in which both leaders were killed. To this painting, exhibited at the Royal Academy in 1826, were attached the lines:

To drive the deere with hound and horne
Erle Percy took his way;
The chiefest harts in Chevy Chase
To kill and beare away.

It is possible that Landseer was introduced to the poem by Sir Walter Scott whom he visited at Abbotsford in 1824. This painting shows very clearly the influence of Rubens upon the young Landseer, the head of the man blowing the horn being a direct quotation from that painter, and the composition being based upon the *Wolf and Fox Hunt*, now in the Metropolitan Museum. [PLATE 63]

BEN MARSHALL (1767–1835). Born in Leicestershire, his master being Francis Lemuel Abbott. He is said to have turned from portrait to animal painting as a result of seeing Gilpin's *The Death of a Fox*. From 1796 his work was regularly published in the *Sporting Magazine*, for which he also wrote articles under the psuedonym 'Observator'. In

1812 he moved from London to Newmarket, where he remained until 1835. In 1819 a serious coaching accident did much to destroy his health and his powers. He exhibited only occasionally at the Royal Academy. Apart from a number of portraits, Marshall painted mainly pictures of horses, including many of the most famous of his day, and scenes of hunting and horse-racing.

Mr Charles Bunbury's 'Eleanor' (Saunders up) and Mr Mellish's 'Surprise'. Oil on canvas. 43½ × 60. Coll. Stephen C. Clarke, Jnr.

Eleanor won the Derby and the Oaks in 1801. [PLATE 44]

The Malcolm Arabian. Oil on canvas. 36 × 48. Coll. unknown.

This animal was the property of George IV, who wished to improve the breed of horses by keeping it in public service at a small fee. [PLATE 45]

William Fermor and his Hounds at Tusmore. Oil on canvas. 57 × 81 Coll. Major R. Macdonald-Buchanan.

This painting dates from the last period of Marshall's life. [PLATE 46]

Fighting Cocks. Oil on canvas. 35 × 41. Coll. Sir Alfred H. Aykroyd, Bart. [PLATE 47]

GEORGE MORLAND (1763–1804). Born in London, the son of a painter. He began to draw at a very early age and exhibited at the Royal Academy at the age of ten. After an apprenticeship with his father, he set up on his own in 1784, but soon became a slave to the picture dealer in whose house he lodged. His companions were said to have been 'ostlers, potboys, horse-jockeys, money lenders, pawnbrokers, punks and pugilists'. His excesses led him into debt and having eluded his debtors for some time by constantly changing his lodgings, he was finally arrested in 1799. He painted at an extraordinary speed and his production was very great, though his pictures were constantly copied and forged, or completed by others. About two hundred and fifty engravings after his pictures appeared during his lifetime, many by his brothers-in-law, William and James Ward.

A Cat. Oil on canvas. 12 × 15. Signed and dated 1792. Coll. Mrs Savill.

This picture almost certainly represents Morland's own cat, as the same animal appears in a painting of Mrs Morland putting the children to bed (Coll. Capt. E. C. Palmer). [PLATE 42]

Outside a Stable. Oil on canvas. $58\frac{1}{2} \times 80\frac{1}{4}$. Coll. unknown.
This picture was exhibited at the R.A. in 1793. [PLATE 43]

PHILIP REINAGLE (1749–1833). A pupil of Alan Ramsay and a student at the Royal Academy Schools. He began his career as a portrait painter but soon turned his attention to animal painting. He was also a skilful copyist of the Dutch seventeenth-century masters of landscape and cattle. He made drawings for Thornton's *New Illustration of the Sexual System of Linnaeus* and *Philosophy of Botany*.

Portrait of a Setter. Oil on canvas. $44\frac{1}{2} \times 60$. Coll. Messrs Arthur Ackermann and Son, Ltd. [PLATE 37]

A Fox's Mask. Oil on canvas. Coll. unknown. [PLATE 38]

THOMAS ROWLANDSON (1756–1827)

Watering Horses. Watercolour. 6×9. Coll. Gilbert Davis. [PLATE 40]

The Betting Post. Watercolour. 10×14. Coll. Gilbert Davis. [PLATE 41]

FRANCIS SARTORIUS (1734–1804). Son of John Sartorius, the first representative of four generations of animal painters. His earliest important picture was a portrait of the Duke of Grafton's racehorse *Antinous*, also painted by Stubbs. Sartorius was a prolific painter of horse portraits and he is said to have depicted the great *Eclipse* more often than any other artist.

Two Horses in Harness. Oil on canvas. $25\frac{1}{8} \times 36$. Coll. Mr and Mrs S. B. D. Hood. [PLATE 36]

JAMES SEYMOUR (1702–52). The son of James Seymour, a banker, amateur artist and friend of Lely and Wren. He won a considerable reputation for his portraits of horses and for his pictures of horse-racing and hunting. Among his many distinguished patrons was Charles Seymour, 3rd Duke of Somerset, who employed him to decorate a room at Petworth with portraits of his horses.

Horse and Jockey. Red chalk. $6\frac{7}{8} \times 9\frac{3}{16}$. Witt Collection, Courtauld Institute. [PLATE 17]

The Duke of Grafton's Running Horses. Oil on canvas. Coll. unknown. [PLATE 18]

GEORGE STUBBS (1724–1806). Born in Liverpool, the son of a tanner. His interest in anatomy began before he was ten years old, but his only training as a painter, under Hamlet Winstanley at the age of fifteen, lasted not more than a few weeks. Between 1744 and 1755 he worked mainly as a portrait painter in the north of England. He visited Italy in 1754. From 1760 his home was in London. He was the author and illustrator of two works on anatomy: *The Anatomy of the Horse* (1766) and *A Comparative Anatomical Exposition of the Structure of the Human Body with that of a Tiger and a Common Fowl*, the latter left incomplete at his death. He also made the illustrations for John Burton's *An Essay towards a Complete New System of Midwifery* (1751). He painted horses, dogs and many species of wild animals, portraits and conversation pieces, scenes of country life, hunting, racing, and shooting. In addition to painting in oils he worked in enamel colour on copper and on stoneware plaques made for him by Josiah Wedgwood, by whom he was employed as a modeller. He also published a number of engravings. He was Treasurer (1772) and Director (1773) of the Free Society of Artists and was elected A.R.A. in 1780. His natural son, George Townley Stubbs, was a painter and engraver.

An Indian Rhinoceros. Oil on canvas. 27½ × 36½. Coll. Hunterian Collection, Royal College of Surgeons.

This picture with others (see Plate 26) was commissioned by the surgeon and anatomist, John Hunter (1728–93) for inclusion in his famous and revolutionary museum formed to demonstrate the anatomy and physiology of the whole animal kingdom. The rhinoceros is of the same species as that drawn and engraved by Dürer, but Stubbs's painting is probably the first accurate representation of the creature. This specimen was exhibited in 1772 at Pidcock's menagerie, Spring Gardens and a number of the drawings which the artist made from it were included in the sale of his effects. (See note to Plate 6.)

[PLATE I, FACING P. 16]

Mares and Foals in a Landscape. Oil on canvas. 39 × 74. Coll. National Trust, Ascott Collection.

Stubbs painted at least half a dozen pictures of this character, in two of which (Fitzwilliam Collection) the horses are arranged against a plain, neutral background. There is no reason to suppose that these pictures were commissioned as a record of particular animals and they are probably variations upon a theme of Stubbs's invention. This type of composition was adopted by other painters of the century, among them Gilpin and Boultbee. [PLATE VI, FACING P. 57]

Orinoco, with a Dog. Oil on panel. 22 × 28. Signed and dated 1780. Coll. Major J. B. Walker. [PLATE 19]

A Cheetah (detail). Oil on canvas. Length 60 in. approx. Coll. Sir George Pigot Bart.

This detail is taken from a large painting (71 × 107) which was commissioned by Sir George Pigot (1719–1777) to commemorate the gift of this animal to George III, during the former's second period of office as Governor of Madras (1775–1777). The cheetah was sent to England in the charge of two Indian servants who are also shown in the picture and was set to hunt a stag in Windsor Park. The crowd of spectators was so great that the creature became too frightened to respond. [PLATE 20]

Prancing Horse and two Dogs. Oil on canvas. 40 × 50. Signed and dated 1791. Coll. unknown. [PLATE 21]

A Horse frightened by a Lion. Oil on canvas. 40 × 50. Signed and dated 1770. Coll. Walker Art Gallery, Liverpool.

This is one of a sequence of three scenes representing a lion attacking a horse of which Stubbs made several versions in oil and enamel colour. The subjects were also engraved, both by himself and by others. The manuscript memoir of the painter by his friend, Ozias Humphry, states that he saw such an incident in Morocco during his return from Italy (*c.* 1755). These pictures were perhaps the most famous and popular of his works and the French painter Géricault made a copy, now in the Louvre, of the last scene of the series. [PLATE 22]

The Lincolnshire Ox. Oil on panel. 26 × 38. Coll. Walker Art Gallery, Liverpool.

This famous animal was bred in 1782 at Gedney, Lincs, by John Gibbons of Little Sutton, and achieved a height of 19 hands. It was exhibited at the Lyceum in the Strand in 1790. The picture, for which Stubbs was paid £64 12s 6d, includes a portrait of Sutton and of a fighting cock in a setting which probably represents St James's Park. [PLATE 24]

A Tiger. Oil on canvas. 27½ × 35. Coll. Temple Newsam House, Leeds. [PLATE 25]

Baboon and Albino Macaque Monkey. Oil on panel. 26 × 38. Coll. Hunterian Collection, Royal College of Surgeons.

This picture is another of those painted by Stubbs for John Hunter. [PLATE 26]

Portrait of a Foxhound, Ringwood. Oil on canvas. 40 × 50. Signed and dated 1772. Coll. The Earl of Yarborough. [PLATE 27]

Drawing for 'The Anatomy of the Horse'. Black chalk. 18½ × 11½. Coll. Royal Academy of Arts.

This is one of the drawings made by Stubbs in 1759–60 at the farmhouse at Horkstow in Lincolnshire, where he worked on the dissections for his 'Anatomy of the Horse'. He rigged the carcases of the horses on a tackle of hooks and bars attached to the ceiling and arranged their legs in suitable positions on a wooden plank underneath. As he cut his way towards the skeleton, injecting the veins and blood vessels with tallow, he made drawings not only of the whole animal, but of details as well. As he could find no engraver who would reproduce his illustrations, he was forced to do the work himself and the publication was delayed until 1766. The work had an immediate success and one of the most famous anatomists of the time, the Dutchman, Petrus Camper, wrote, 'I am amazed to meet in the same person so great an anatomist, so accurate a painter and so excellent an engraver.' The eighteen drawings in the library of the Royal Academy once belonged to Sir Edwin Landseer. [PLATE 28]

JAMES WARD (1769–1859). Born in London, Ward studied engraving under J. R. Smith and in 1783 became apprenticed to his elder brother the engraver, William Ward. His early paintings were much influenced in style and subject by his brother-in-law George Morland. In 1794 he was appointed painter and mezzotint engraver to the Prince of Wales, was elected A.R.A. in 1807 and R.A. in 1811. In 1800 he was commissioned jointly by the Agricultural Society and the printseller Boydell to paint a series of 200 portraits illustrating the representative breeds of cattle, pigs, and sheep in Great Britain. This enterprise, however, like so many others in which he was concerned, ended in failure largely due to his neurotic and undependable personality. In 1803 he saw Rubens *A View of the Chateau de Steen*, then in the possession of Sir George Beaumont, a work which he tried to surpass in his own *The Fighting Bulls at St Donat's Castle*. Between 1815 and 1821 he gave much of his time to a vast allegorical composition commemorating Wellington's victory at Waterloo, his design for which had won a prize offered by the British Institution. After endless trials and labours the picture was exhibited in 1822, but in view of the criticism it received was never properly housed and has since disappeared. Ward's production of paintings and drawings was vast and various, for although primarily an animal painter he worked in almost every genre. Apart from his portraits of wild and domestic animals, he painted landscapes, religious subjects, portraits, conversation pieces, and history pictures.

Horses Surprised by Wolves. Oil on canvas. Signed and dated 1842. 28¾ × 54. Coll. Tate Gallery.

This picture, one of Ward's most intricate and sophisticated compositions, is by no means typical of his style at this period.

[PLATE III, FACING P. 32]

Sheep, and a Shorn-Fleece. Oil on canvas. 10¼ × 13¼. Coll. Peter Cochrane, Esq.

This picture may have been a study for a picture of sheep shearing exhibited at the Academy in 1846. Ward also made portraits of sheep of particular breeds, such as Merino, Durham, Romney Marsh, Shropshire, New Leicester. [PLATE IV, FACING P. 41]

L'Amour de Cheval. Oil on canvas. 56 × 83. Coll. Tate Gallery. (Reproduced by courtesy of the Trustees.)

Exhibited at the Royal Academy in 1828. [PLATE 48]

A Stag in an Open Landscape. Oil on canvas. 23 × 26. Signed and dated 1838. Col. H. Noel Whiting.

Few pictures of stags, apart from hunting subjects, occur in English art before 1800, but they were to become the most popular subject of nineteenth-century animal painting, representing as they do a dignified, picturesque and vulnerable wildness, easily interpreted in terms of human emotion. [PLATE 49]

The Descent of the Swan. Oil on panel. 13½ × 12. Coll. H. Noel Whiting.

This painting (which once belonged to the Victorian animal painter, Briton Riviere) was exhibited at the Royal Academy in 1817 and was later used as an illustration to 'The Social Day', a poem in four cantos by the auctioneer, Peter Coxe. [PLATE 50]

Col. Platoff on his Charger. Oil on canvas. 55 × 43½. Coll. Duke of Northumberland.

This picture was exhibited at the Royal Academy in 1815, and makes an interesting comparison with Géricault's equestrian paintings of officers in the Napoleonic armies. [PLATE 51]

The Fall of Phaeton. Oil on canvas. 49 × 39⅛. Coll. Lord Camrose.

Several versions of this subject are recorded, but the one illustrated would appear to be a finished sketch. The story of Phaeton is one which appealed to those animal painters who wished to find a means of approaching the dignity of a history painter, and both Stubbs and Gilpin painted scenes from this legend. [PLATE 52]

Horse and Boa-constrictor. Oil on canvas. Coll. unknown.

This painting is the finished sketch for a picture submitted to the Roya Academy in 1803. Its rejection provoked Ward to cut himself off from the Academy for four years. The large picture was subsequently lost in a shipwreck on its way to an exhibition in the United States in 1822.

[PLATE 53]

Persian Greyhounds. Oil on canvas. 40×50. Coll. Sidney F. Sabin.

This picture is almost certainly the one exhibited at the British Institution in 1807. [PLATE 54]

A Bat. Watercolour. $7\frac{3}{4} \times 8\frac{3}{4}$. Witt Collection, Courtauld Institute.

[PLATE 55]

Portrait of a Hereford Bull. Oil on panel. Coll. Walker Galleries.

This is one of the paintings which resulted from the commission given to Ward by the Agricultural Society and Boydell. (See biographical note). [PLATE 56]

THOMAS WEAVER (1774–1843). A painter of all kinds of animal subjects, but particularly noted for his portraits of pedigree cattle. Among his early patrons was Thomas Coke of Holkham.

A White Short Horned Heifer. Coloured mezzotint by William Ward after Thomas Weaver. $17\frac{7}{8} \times 23\frac{3}{4}$. Dated 1811.

This animal was bred by Robert Colling, one of the pioneers in the scientific breeding of farm stock. [PLATE 57]

JOHN WOOTTON (1678?–1765). Wootton's first master was Jan Wyck, a painter of hunting and battle scenes, and he later assisted the landscape painter, Siberechts. He first became known at Newmarket and painted all the most famous racehorses of his time. Among his patrons was the 3rd Duke of Beaufort, who enabled him to study in Rome. Besides his portraits of horses and dogs, he painted battle and hunting pictures and equestrian portraits, while in later life he devoted himself mainly to landscape, in the manner of Claude and Gaspard Poussin. He also painted horses for the portraitist, Michael Dahl. He was responsible for the illustrations in the first volume of Gay's *Fables.* His best work may be seen at Althorp, Longleat, and Welbeck.

A Stallion Fight. Oil on canvas. 102×144. Coll. Marquis of Bath.

This is the smallest of the group of Woottons at Longleat commissioned by the 2nd Viscount Weymouth, the rest being hunting scenes. The stable boy on the right, who was killed in the fight, appears in all the pictures. He had been found abandoned on the estate as an infant.

[PLATE 13]

Members of the Beaufort Hunt. Oil on canvas. 78 × 95. Coll. Tate Gallery. (Reproduced by courtesy of the Trustees.)

This painting shows the 3rd Earl of Litchfield, on horseback, and his uncle, the 4th Earl, with a gun, in the coats of the Beaufort Hunt.

[PLATE 14]

Portrait of a Spotted Stallion. Oil on canvas. 53½ × 66½. Coll. Messrs Arthur Ackermann and Son, Ltd. [PLATE 15]

Newmarket Heath. Oil on canvas. 40 × 50. Coll. Lord Fairhaven.

The picture shows Warren Hill, the King's chair, and, watching the horses on the right, Tregonwell Frampton, the trainer of the royal horses at Newmarket. [PLATE 16]

BIBLIOGRAPHY

THE literature of English animal painting is not only limited, but is by no means reliable. The most useful work has been done by the late Walter Shaw Sparrow, and the following books by him have been found most valuable, if critically used, in the preparation of the present essay:

British Sporting Artists (1922).
A Book of Sporting Painters (1931).
British Farm Animals in prints and paintings (Walker's Quarterly, 1932).

An earlier but less detailed work than these was Sir Walter Gilbey's

The Animal Painters of England from the year 1650 (1889).

Among the comparatively few monographs on the professional animal painters are the following:

HENRY ALKEN: *The Alken Family*. W. Shaw Sparrow (1927).
FRANCIS BARLOW: The fullest accounts of his career occur in Shaw Sparrow and in W. A. Baillie-Grohmann's *Sport in Art* (n.d.).
THOMAS BEWICK: Apart from his own delightful memoir there are studies by Austin Dobson (1884), D. Croal Thomson (1930), on the watercolours, Graham Reynolds (1949), Montague Weekley (1953), and Reynolds Stone (1954).
JOHN FERNELEY: *The Melton Mowbray of John Ferneley*. Guy Paget (1931).
SIR EDWIN LANDSEER: Studies by F. G. Stephens (1874), Algernon Graves (1876), and J. B. Manson (1922).
BEN MARSHALL: *George Stubbs and Ben Marshall*. W. Shaw Sparrow (1929).
GEORGE MORLAND: Biographies or studies by J. Hassell (1806), George Dawe (1807), G. C. Williamson (1904), Sir W. Gilbey, and E. D. Cuming (1907).
GEORGE STUBBS: *Memoirs of Thomas Dodd, William Upcott and George Stubbs*. Joseph Mayer (1879). Studies by Sir Walter Gilbey (1898), W. Shaw Sparrow (1929), Geoffrey Grigson (in The Harp of Æeolus, 1947), Basil Taylor (*Image*, No. 3, 1949–50) on the engraved work, anatomical illustrations and drawings. The present author is engaged on a life of Stubbs with a catalogue of his work.
JAMES WARD: Studies by Julia Frankau (1904) and C. Reginald Grundy (1909).

The files of *The Field, Country Life*, and *The Connoisseur* should also be consulted. Other books which have been consulted include:

A History of the English Turf, by Sir Theodore Cook (n.d.).
The Origin and Influence of the Thoroughbred Horse, by William Ridgeway (1906).
Histoire des Menageries, by J. Loisel (1912).
A History of Comparative Anatomy, by F. J. Cole (1944).

Although I have not, in this essay, been concerned with the special question of the sporting print, I should here mention *The Story of British Sporting Prints*. Captain Harry Siltzer (new ed., 1927).

INDEX

The following is a list of the English painters mentioned in the tex and in the notes to the plates, together with those foreign animal painters who worked in England. Main entries are printed in italics.

Anonymous: Portrait of Sir John Harington's Dog, Bungey (or Bungy).
Coll. Lord Fairhaven

(a) Francis Barlow: Hare and Hounds (detail). *Coll. Lord Onslow*

(b) Francis Barlow: Hare-hunting. *Ashmolean Museum*

Francis Barlow: Fish. *Coll. Unknown*

Francis Barlow: Cat and Kittens. *Witt Collection, Courtauld Institute*

Francis Barlow: The Decoy at Pyrford at Sunset with Waterfowl startled by a Bird of Prey. *Coll. Lord Onslow*

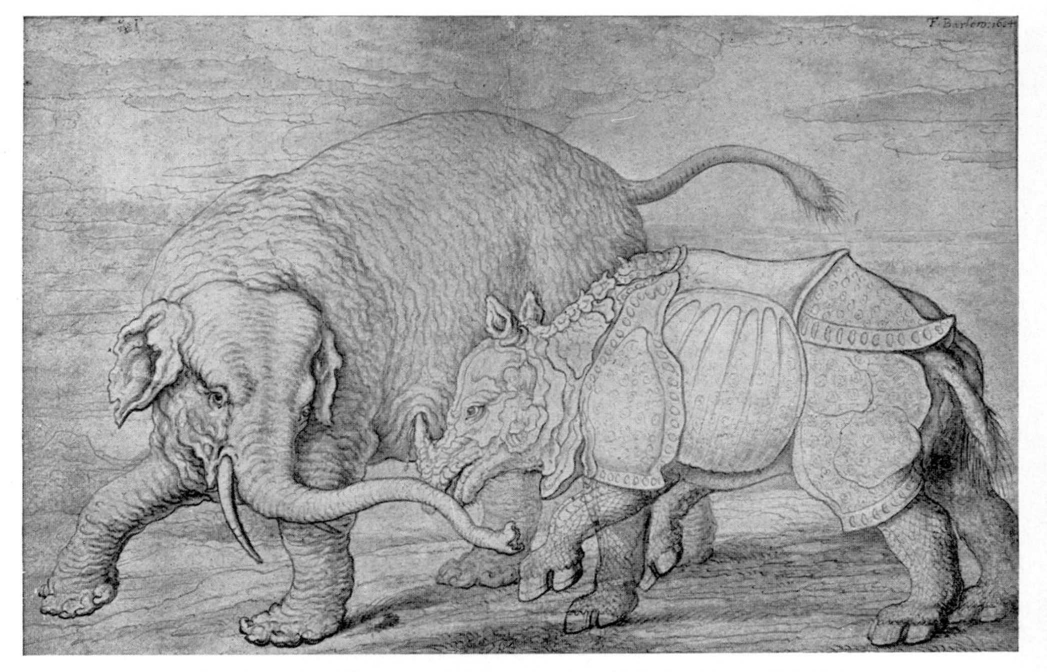

Francis Barlow: Elephant and Rhinoceros. *Witt Collection, Courtauld Institute*

Abraham van Diepenbeck: One of the Duke of Newcastle's Horses, with a View of Welbeck. *Coll. Duke of Portland*

Marmaduke Cradock: Fighting Cock, four years old, belonging to Baron Hollis.
Coll. Unknown

William Hogarth: The Painter and his Pug. *Tate Gallery*

William Hogarth: A Cat, detail from 'The Graham Children'.
Tate Gallery

William Hogarth: Detail from 'A Rake's Progress, Scene V'.
Sir John Soane's Museum

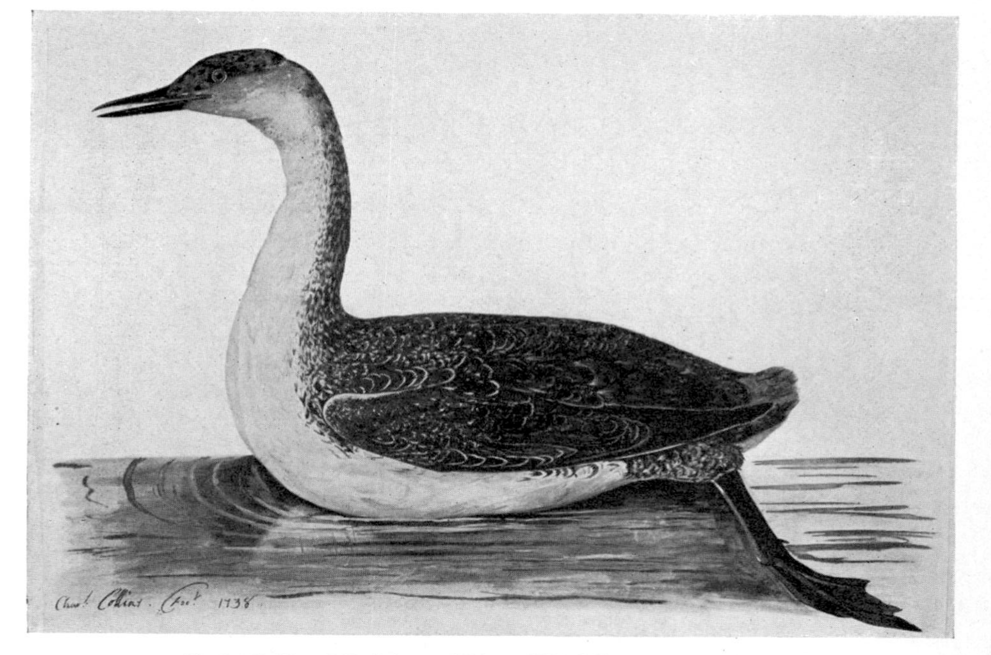

Charles Collins: A Red-throated Diver. *Witt Collection, Courtauld Institute*

John Wootton: A Stallion Fight. *Coll. Marquis of Bath*

John Wootton: Members of the Beaufort Hunt. *Tate Gallery*

John Wootton: Portrait of a Spotted Stallion. *Coll. Messrs Arthur Ackermann & Son Ltd*

John Wootton: Newmarket Heath. *Coll. Lord Fairhaven*

James Seymour: Horse and Jockey. *Witt Collection, Courtauld Institute*

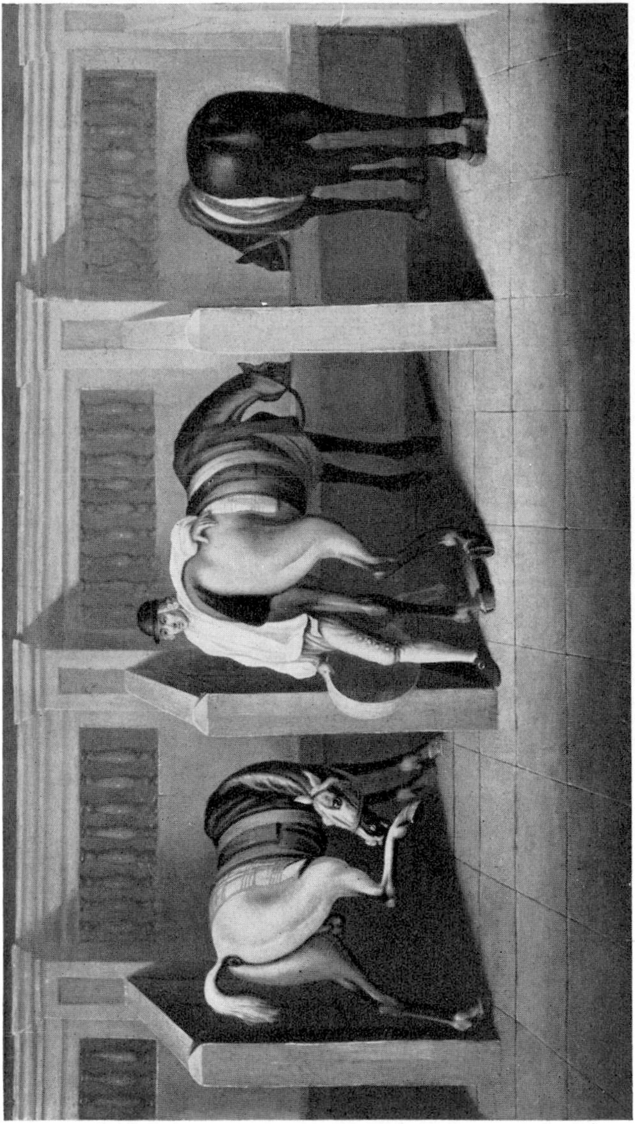

James Seymour: The Duke of Grafton's Running Horses. *Coll. Unknown*

George Stubbs: Orinoco, with a Dog. *Coll. Major J.B. Walker*

George Stubbs: A Cheetah (detail). *Coll. Sir George Pigot, Bart*

George Stubbs: Prancing Horse and two Dogs. *Coll. Unknown*

George Stubbs: A Horse frightened by a Lion. *Walker Art Gallery, Liverpool*

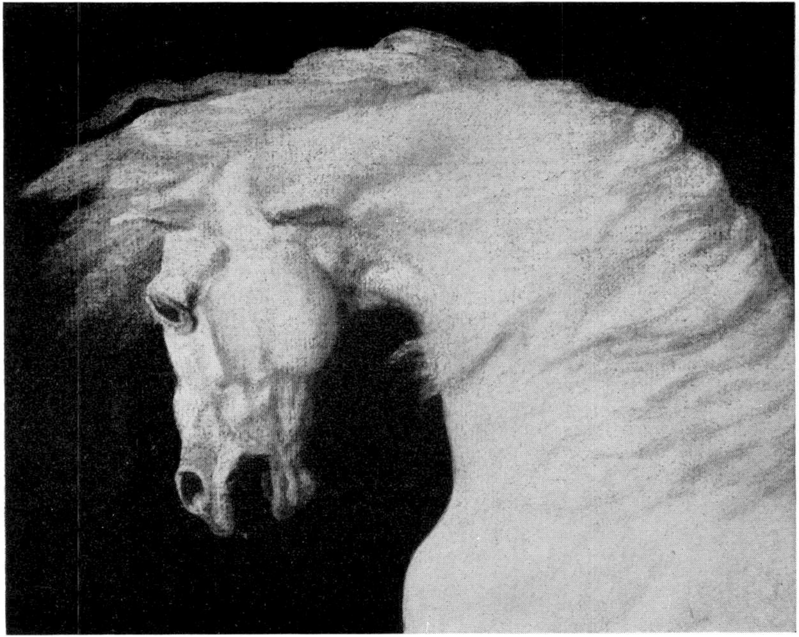

Detail of plate 22

George Stubbs: The Lincolnshire Ox. *Walker Art Gallery, Liverpool*

George Stubbs: A Tiger. *Temple Newsam House, Leeds*

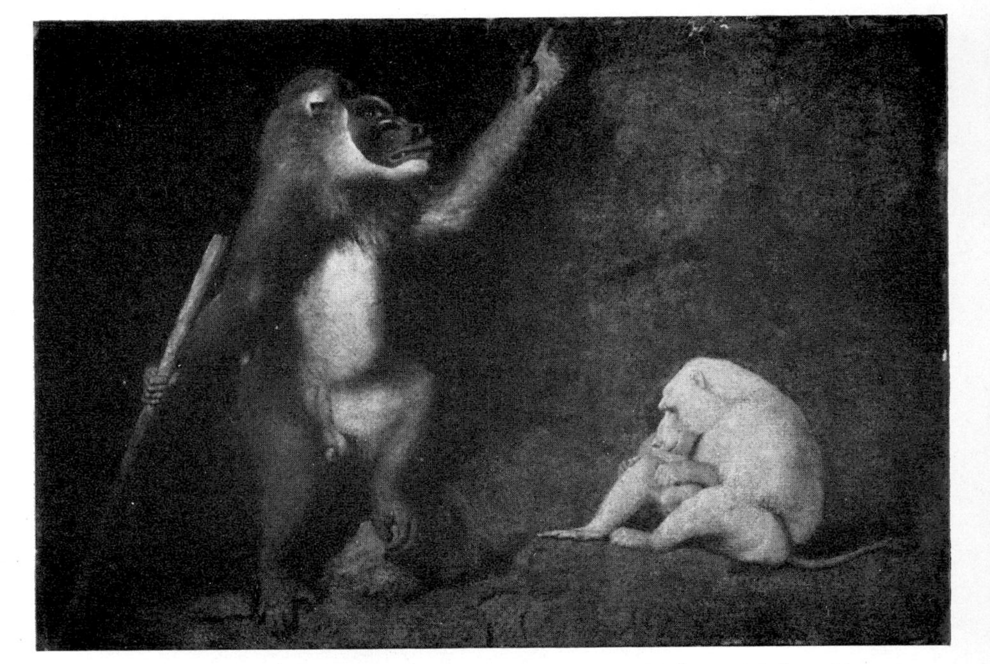

George Stubbs: Baboon and Albino Macaque Monkey. *Hunterian Coll., Royal College of Surgeons*

George Stubbs: Portrait of a Foxhound, Ringwood. *Coll. The Earl of Yarborough*

George Stubbs: Drawing for 'The Anatomy of the Horse'. *Royal Academy of Arts*

Thomas Gainsborough: Portrait of a Dog, Bumper. *Coll. Sir Edmund Bacon*

Thomas Gainsborough: Study of an Old Horse. *Tate Gallery*

Sawrey Gilpin: Horses frightened in a Thunderstorm. *Royal Academy of Arts*

Sawrey Gilpin: Gulliver describing Fortification to the Horses. *York Art Gallery*

Sawrey Gilpin: The Election of Darius. *York Art Gallery*

Sawrey Gilpin: Bears. *Witt Collection, Courtauld Institute*

Sawrey Gilpin: A Grey Arab Horse. *Fitzwilliam Museum, Cambridge*

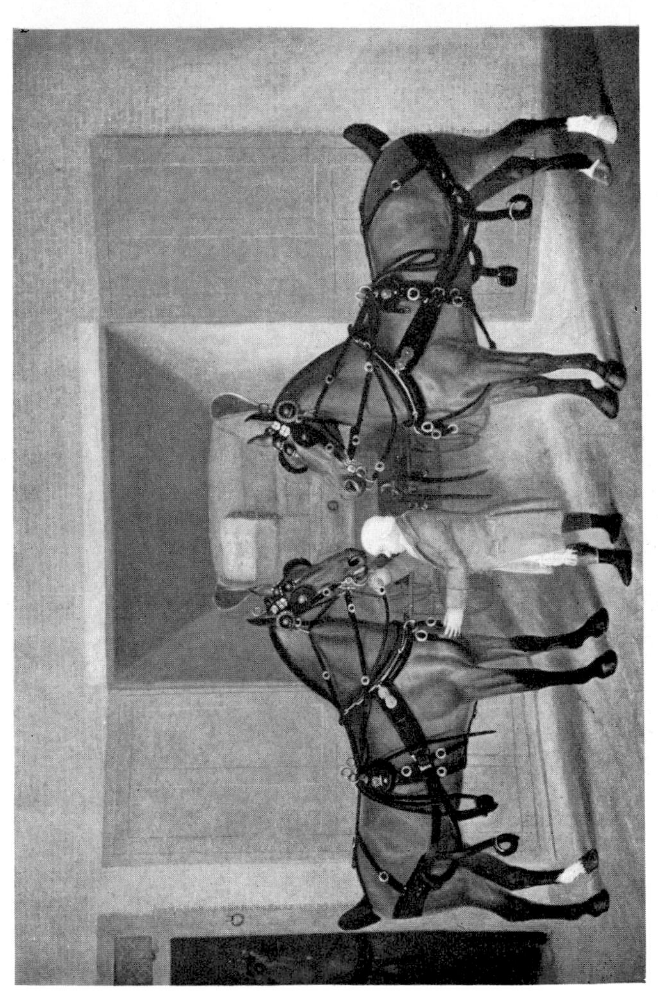

Francis Sartorius: Two Horses in Harness. *Coll. Mr and Mrs S. B. D. Hood*

Philip Reinagle: Portrait of a Setter. *Coll. Messrs Arthur Ackermann & Son Ltd*

Philip Reinagle: A Fox's Mask. *Coll. Unknown*

Thomas Bewick: A Starling. *Witt Collection, Courtauld Institute*

Thomas Rowlandson: Watering Horses. *Coll. Gilbert Davis*

Thomas Rowlandson: The Betting Post. *Coll. Gilbert Davis*

George Morland: A Cat. *Coll. Mrs Savill*

George Morland: Outside a Stable. *Coll. Unknown*

Ben Marshall: Mr Charles Bunbury's 'Eleanor' (Saunders Up) and Mr Mellish's 'Surprise'.
Coll. Stephen C. Clarke, Jnr

Ben Marshall: The Malcolm Arabian. *Coll. Unknown*

Ben Marshall: William Fermor and his Hounds at Tusmore. *Coll. Major R. Macdonald-Buchanan*

Ben Marshall: Fighting Cocks. *Coll. Sir Alfred H. Aykroyd, Bart*

James Ward: L'Amour de Cheval. *Tate Gallery*

James Ward: A Stag in an Open Landscape. *Coll. H. Noel Whiting*

James Ward: The Descent of the Swan. *Coll. H. Noel Whiting*

James Ward: Col. Platoff on his Charger. *Coll. Duke of Northumberland*

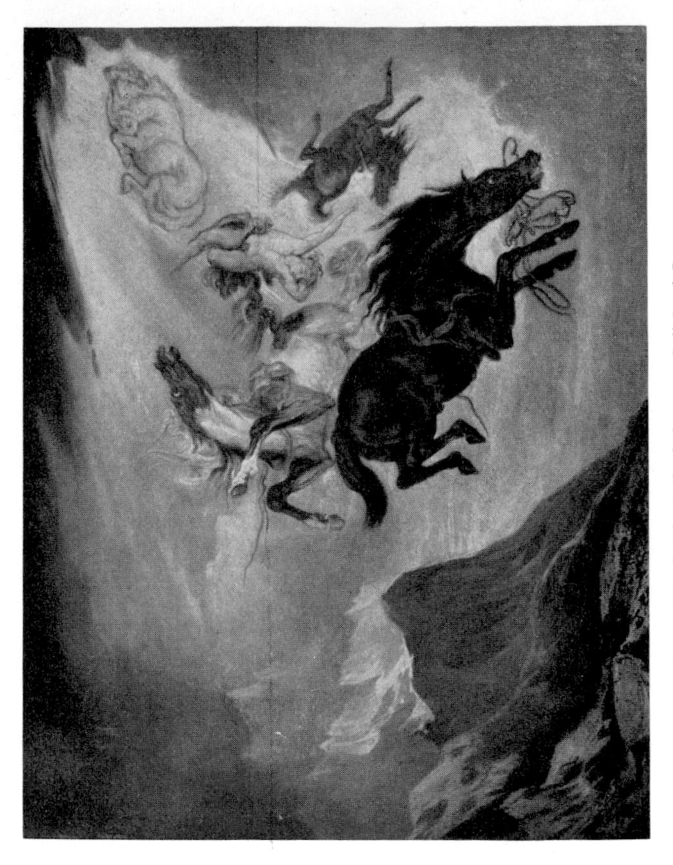

James Ward: The Fall of Phaeton. *Coll. Lord Camrose*

James Ward: Horse and Boa-Constrictor. *Coll. Unknown*

James Ward: Persian Greyhounds. *Coll. Sidney F. Sabin*

James Ward: A Bat. *Witt Collection, Courtauld Institute*

James Ward: A Hereford Bull. *Coll. Unknown*

Thomas Weaver: A White Short Horned Heifer

Luke Clennell: Baggage Waggons in a Storm. *Coll. Unknown*

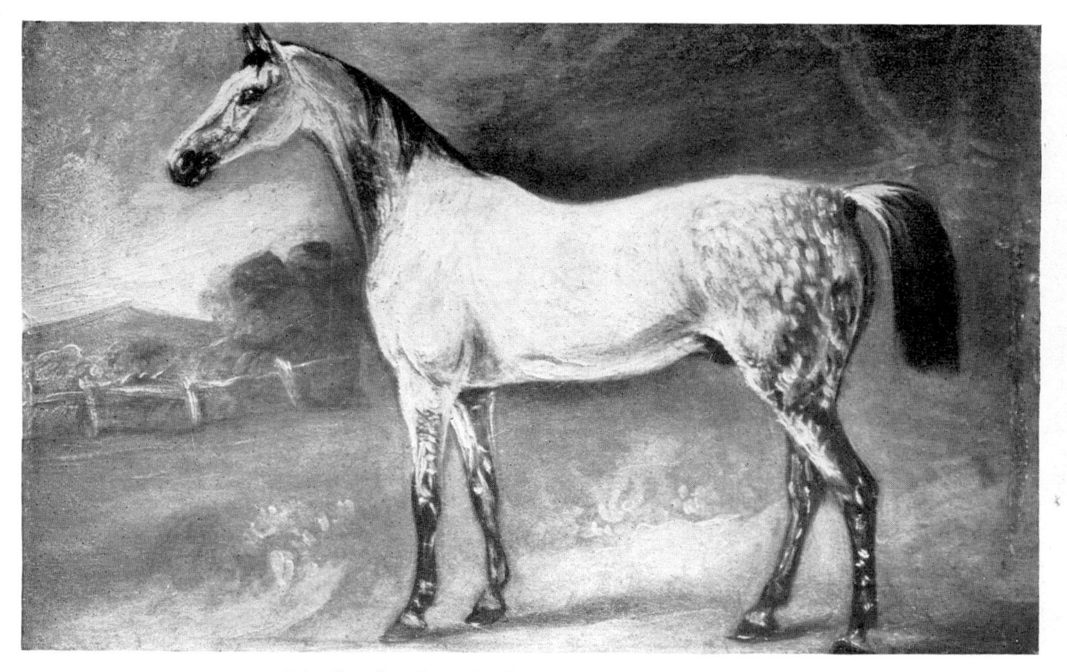

John Ferneley: Portrait of a Hunter. *Coll. Sidney F. Sabin*

Henry Alken: The Melton Hunt, 1826: Getting Away. *Coll. Unknown*

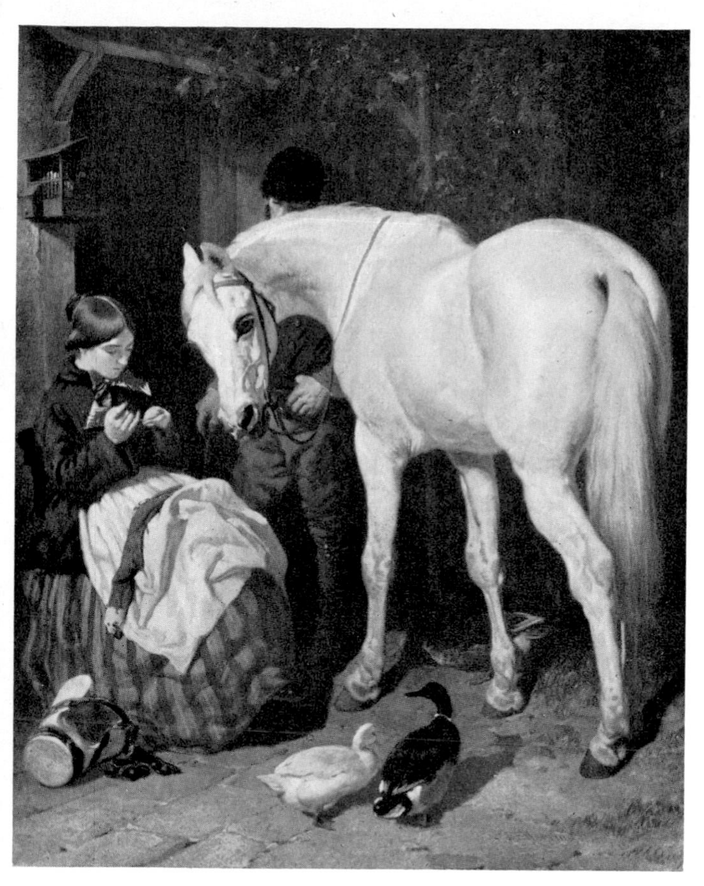

John Frederick Herring: White Horse outside a Cottage. *Private Collection*

J. L. Agasse: The Nubian Giraffe.
Reproduced by gracious permission of Her Majesty the Queen

Sir Edward Landseer: The Hunting of Chevy Chase.
National Art-Collections Fund

William Holman Hunt: Detail from 'The Hireling Shepherd'.
Manchester City Art Gallery